OPERATION BAGRATION

Ian Baxter is a military historian who specialises in German twentieth century military history. He has written more than twenty books including Into the Abyss: The Last Years of the Waffen-SS, From Retreat to Defeat: The Last Years of the German Army on the Eastern Front, Poland – The Eighteen Day Victory March, Panzers In North Africa, The Red Army at Stalingrad, and German Guns of the Third Reich, as well as contributing over 100 articles to a range of well-known military periodicals. He currently lives in Essex with Michelle and son Felix.

Operation Bagration – the Russian codename for the 1944 summer offensive which led to the complete annihilation of Army Group Centre – was without doubt the most devastating defeat ever experienced by the German Army during the Second World War. Yet this mammoth offensive has for years been completely overshadowed by the Normandy campaign, which was unleashed just three weeks prior to Bagration along the shores of northern France.

The battle which the German forces of Army Group Centre endured on the Eastern Front that fateful summer was more catastrophic than that experienced on the Western Front, but the English-speaking world remains largely ignorant of its details. This book reveals the lesser-known battle in the East, and demonstrates the gallantry and self-sacrifice of the German forces against overwhelming odds.

Drawing on rare and previously unpublished photographs accompanied by in-depth captions, the book vividly describes how the German forces of Army Group Centre endured a massive Russian offensive three years to the day after Germany's 1941 invasion of the Soviet Union. Fighting over many of the same battlefields, it reveals how scores of German troops were urged on by their Führer to defend their positions to the death in a desperate attempt to prevent the mighty Red Army forces from recapturing Byelorussia, the last bastion of defence for the Germans before Poland. The Bagration offensive was a bloodthirsty battle of attrition which resulted in a catastrophe of unbelievable proportions.

Throughout the book the author provides an absorbing analysis of this traumatic battle and shows how German soldiers continued to fight to the bitter end amidst the constant hammer blows of ground and aerial bombardment, and endless armoured and infantry attacks. Although many German units continued to wage a grim and bitter defence the Red Army swamped the already overstretched front lines. The Soviets punched massive holes in the disintegrating defences almost everywhere, letting through a seemingly unstoppable flood, pushing apart and encircling many precious German Panzer and infantry divisions. In the end Bagration cost the Wehrmacht more men and material than the catastrophe at Stalingrad sixteen months earlier. The shattering defeat of Army Group Centre resulted in the loss of over 300,000 men, and witnessed Soviet forces pushing exhausted German remnants out of Russia and through Poland to the gates of Warsaw.

OPERATION BAGRATION

THE DESTRUCTION OF ARMY GROUP CENTRE
JUNE-JULY 1944

A Photographic History

Ian Baxter

Helion & Company Ltd

Helion & Company Limited
26 Willow Road
Solihull
West Midlands
B91 1UE
England
Tel. 0121 705 3393
Fax 0121 711 4075
Email: publishing@helion.co.uk
Website: http://www.helion.co.uk

Published by Helion & Company 2007

Designed and typeset by Helion & Company Limited, Solihull, West Midlands
Cover designed by Bookcraft Limited, Stroud, Gloucestershire
Printed by Cromwell Press Ltd, Trowbridge, Wiltshire

Text © Ian Baxter 2007
Photographs © History in the Making Archive (HITM) unless otherwise credited.
Map © Helion & Company Ltd. The publishers would like readers to note that the map is substantially based on that
appearing on page 317 of Earl F. Ziemke's 'Stalingrad to Berlin: the German Defeat in the East' (Washington DC:
U.S. Army Centre of Military History, 1968). Due acknowledgment is hereby given to the copyright holders.

Front cover images: During the battle of Vitebsk a German Pak crew can be seen
in the thick of battle trying to defend their positions.

ISBN 978 1 906033 09 5

British Library Cataloguing-in-Publication Data.
A catalogue record for this book is available from the British Library.

For details of other military history titles published by Helion & Company Limited contact the above address, or visit
our website: http://www.helion.co.uk.

We always welcome receiving book proposals from prospective authors.

Contents

Photographic acknowledgements viii

Introduction ix

Prologue: Prelude to Destruction: Army Group Centre 1941–44 1

Part I
Operation Bagration unleashed 22–28 June 1944 10

Part II
Fighting for Survival 29 June–6 July 1944 47

Part III
Destruction 6–13 July 1944 81

Aftermath 107

Appendices
I   German Organisation 1944 109
II   Hitler's Operation Order No. 8 115
III Army Group Centre Order of Battle 15 June 1944 117
IV   Army Group Centre Order of Battle 23 June 1944 118
V   Red Army Order of Battle 23 June 1944 119
VI   Army Group Centre Order of Battle 15 July 1944 123
VII Army Group Centre Order of Battle 19 July 1944 124
VIII Table of Ranks 125

Bibliography 127

Photographic Acknowledgements

It is with the greatest pleasure that I use this opportunity on concluding this book to thank those who helped make this volume possible. My expression of gratitude first goes to my German photographic collector Rolf Halfen. He has been an unfailing source: supplying me with a number of photographs that were obtained from numerous private sources. Throughout the research stage of this book Rolf searched and contacted numerous collectors all over Germany, attempting to find a multitude of interesting and rare photographs.

Further afield in Poland I am also extremely grateful to Marcin Kaludow and Robert Michulec, my Polish photographic specialists, who supplied me with a great variety photographs that they sought from private photographic collections in Poland, Russia and the Ukraine.

Finally, I wish to display my kindness and appreciation to my American photographic collector, Richard White, who supplied me with a number of rare unpublished photographs, especially showing the various Luftwaffe field divisions deployed on the Eastern Front.

Introduction

This book is a unique insight into the greatest military defeat ever experienced by the German Army during World War Two, Bagration being the Russian code-name for the 1944 summer offensive which led to the destruction of Army Group Centre.

Drawing on rare and previously unpublished photographs accompanied by in-depth captions, the book vividly describes how the German forces of Army Group Centre endured a massive Russian offensive three years to the day after Germany's 1941 invasion of the Soviet Union. Fighting over many of the same battlefields, it reveals how scores of German troops fought to the death in a desperate attempt to prevent the mighty Red Army forces from recapturing Byelorussia, the last bastion of defence for the Germans before Poland. The Bagration offensive, in which Army Group Centre was compelled to counter, was a swift and bloodthirsty battle of attrition that resulted in a catastrophe of unbelievable proportions. This study provides an absorbing analysis of this traumatic battle and tells how German soldiers continued to fight to the bitter end, enduring the constant hammer blows of ground and aerial bombardment, and endless armoured and infantry attacks. Although many German units continued to put up a grim and bitter defence, the Red Army had already punched a hole through the front line, allowing an almost unstoppable flood, pushing apart and encircling many precious German Panzer and infantry divisions. In the end Bagration cost the Wehrmacht more men and material than the catastrophe at Stalingrad sixteen months earlier. This shattering defeat of Army Group Centre saw the loss of over 300,000 men and resulted in Soviet forces pushing back exhausted German remnants out of Russia through Poland to the gates of Warsaw.

The destruction of Army Group Centre in the summer of 1944 has been completely overshadowed by the Normandy campaign, which was unleashed just three weeks prior to Bagration along the shores of northern France. The battle which the German forces endured on the Eastern Front that fateful summer was more catastrophic than on the Western Front, yet little is known of the operation. This book reveals the lesser-known battle in the East and highlights the sacrifice of the German forces against overwhelming odds.

Assessment of the German Soldier in 1944

For the German soldier on the Eastern Front, the opening months of 1944 were very gloomy. He had fought desperately to maintain cohesion and hold meagre positions that often saw thousands perish. By May 1944 the German forces were holding a battle line more than 1,400 miles in overall length, which had been severely weakened by the overwhelming strength of the Red Army. To make matters worse, during the first half of 1944 units were no longer being refitted with replacements to compensate for the large losses sustained. Supplies of equipment and ammunition too were so insufficient in some areas of the front that commanders were compelled to issue their men with rations. As a consequence many soldiers had become increasingly aware that they were in the final stages of the war in the East, including battle-hardened combatants. They had also realized that they were now fighting an enemy that was far superior to them in terms of material. As a consequence in a number of sectors of the front soldiers were able to realistically access the war situation, and this in turn managed to save the lives of many that would previously have been killed fighting to the last man.

In spite of the adverse situation in which the German soldier was placed during the first half of 1944, he was still strong and determined to fight with courage and skill. By June 1944 the German soldier had expended considerable combat efforts, although lacking sufficient reconnaissance and the necessary support of tanks and heavy weapons to ensure any type of long-term success. The Red Army constantly outgunned them, and Luftwaffe air support was almost non-existent. The short summer nights, too, had caused considerable problems for the men, for they only had a few hours of darkness in which to conceal their night marches and the construction of field fortifications. Consequently, even before the Red Army summer offensive was finally unleashed across Army Group Centre the front line soldier in the forward combat area was already continuously under fire from Russian artillery and aircraft.

Ultimately, the German soldier in the summer of 1944 was ill prepared against any type of large-scale offensive. The infantry defensive positions relied upon sufficient infantry ammunition supply and the necessary support to ensure that they would able to hold their fortified areas. Without this, the German soldier was doomed. Commanders in the field were fully aware of the significant problems and the difficulties imposed by committing badly-equipped soldiers to defend the depleted lines of defence. However, in the end, they had no other choice than to order their troops to fight with whatever they had at their disposal.

Prologue

Prelude to Destruction: Army Group Centre 1941–44

The history of Army Group Centre began during the summer of 1941 when, on 22 June, the German Army, 3 million strong, began their greatest attack in military history. In Army Group Centre, under the command of Field Marshal Fedor von Bock, 800 Panzers struck across the Russian frontier and within hours the German armoured punch, with brilliant co-ordination of all arms, had pulverised bewildered Russian formations. With nothing but a string of victories behind them by the end of September 1941, Army Group Centre was regrouped for the final assault on Moscow, known as 'Operation Typhoon'. At first the drive to Moscow went well, but by early October the weather began to change as cold and driving rain fell on the troops. Within hours the Russian country-side had been turned into a quagmire, with roads and fields becoming virtually impassable. All roads leading to Moscow had become a boggy swamp. To make matters worse, since 'Typhoon' had begun, Army Group Centre had lost nearly 35,000 men, excluding the sick and injured. Some 240 tanks and heavy artillery pieces with over 800 other vehicles had either developed mechanical problems or been destroyed. Supplies were becoming dangerously low, and fuel and ammunition were hardly adequate to meet the ever-growing demands of the drive to Moscow. Regardless of the dwindling shortages of material Army Group Centre was ordered to continue its march through the freezing arctic conditions. Despair now gripped the front as battered and exhausted troops froze to death in front of the Russian capital. German territorial gains that winter were limited to a forty-mile belt at the approaches to Moscow.

The failure to capture Moscow had been a complete disaster for Army Group Centre. Its forces had altered out of recognition from their victorious summer operations. During early 1942 the Russian offensive petered out. The temperatures rose and Army Group Centre begun to replenish its losses. By June 1942 the preparation of another German summer offensive began. However, instead of attacking Moscow again Army Group Centre consolidated its positions whilst Army Group South advanced to the Caucasus and the Volga. Whilst the battle of Stalingrad raged in the ruins of the city a major Soviet offensive in the Moscow area was unleashed, code-named 'Operation Mars'. The objective was to destroy the Rzhev salient. Already Army Group Centre had heavily fortified the salient with a mass of mine belts, trenches, bunkers, anti-tank guns and machine gun emplacements. The well-constructed road network too allowed the rapid movement of reinforcements to the area. Consequently the Russian offensive failed, suffering heavy casualties. However, three months later in February 1943 the strong lines of defence of Army Group Centre were yet again attacked. The Russians made a co-ordinated assault in the Kursk and northern Army Group Centre areas with the ultimate objective of encircling the Army Group. Again, the Red Army under-estimated the strength and resilience of the German forces in Army Group Centre and eventually the Soviet attacks from Kursk towards Orel failed to make progress. As a result the offensive was called off.

Throughout the first half of 1943 Army Group Centre had maintained more or less the strategic initiative on the Eastern Front. However, by July 1943, when the Germans unleashed their long awaited summer offensive code-named 'Operation Zitadelle', the war in the East changed forever. Within two weeks of the attack, the Red Army had repulsed the German forces with considerable losses. In August, just weeks after the German failure at Kursk, the Red Army counterattacked towards Orel and Kharkov and launched a massive attack against Army Group Centre. For nearly three months the Russians fought a series of heavy clashes against Army Group Centre, managing to recapture Smolensk and the rail junction at Nevel, forcing back the Germans on a broad front. However, the Russian attack soon faltered in the Vitebsk-Orsha-Mogilev area, where almost impregnable lines of defences had been erected by the Germans.

In November 1943 further Red Army assaults were made against Army Group Centre in the Gomel and Orsha areas. The fighting raged for months but the Russians were again unsuccessful against the strong 'Ostwall' defences. During the first months of 1944 Army Group Centre continued to endure repeated heavy attacks, but yet again the Red Army found the mass of well dug-in defences too difficult to break. By the spring of 1944 the Soviet command begun to draw up plans for a massive concentration of forces along the entire frontline in central Russia. The new summer offensive was to be called 'Operation Bagration' and its objective was to annihilate Army Group Centre once and for all.

Army Group Centre Order Of Battle 1941 - 1944

1941

June	9th Army, 4th Army
July	3rd Panzer Group, 9th Army, 4th Army, 2nd Panzer Group, 2nd Army
August	3rd Panzer Group, 9th Army, 2nd Army, Army Group of Guderian
September	3rd Panzer Group, 9th Army, 4th Army, 2nd Panzer Group, 2nd Army
October	9th Army, 4th Army, 2nd Panzer Army, 2nd Army
November	9th Army, 3rd Panzer Group, 4th Army, 2nd Panzer Army, 2nd Army

1942

January	9th Army, 3rd Panzer Army, 4th Panzer Army, 4th Army, 2nd Panzer Army, 2nd Army
February	3rd Panzer Army, 9th Army, 4th Panzer Army, 4th Army, 2nd Panzer Army
May	9th Army, 3rd Panzer Army, 4th Army, 2nd Panzer Army

1943

January	LIX Corps, 9th Army, 3rd Panzer Army, 4th Army, 2nd Panzer Army
February	3rd Panzer Army, 9th Army, 4th Army, 2nd Panzer Army
March	3rd Panzer Army, 9th Army, 4th Army, 2nd Panzer Army, 2nd Army
April	3rd Panzer Army, 4th Army, 2nd Panzer Army, 2nd Army, 9th Army
July	3rd Panzer Army, 4th Army, 2nd Panzer Army, 9th Army, 2nd Army
September	3rd Panzer Army, 4th Army, 9th Army, 2nd Army
November	3rd Panzer Army, 4th Army, 9th Army, 2nd Army, Armed Forces Commander East

1944

January	3rd Panzer Army, 4th Army, 9th Army, 2nd Army
July	3rd Panzer Army, 4th Army, 2nd Army, 9th Army
August	3rd Panzer Army, 4th Army, 4th Army, 2nd Army, IV SS Panzer Corps

Deception Plans

German commanders were fully aware of the dire consequences if Army Group Centre was defeated. They appreciated that if the Russians succeeded here then it would undoubtedly wrench wide open the door to Poland, and then Germany. In spite of being understrength and lacking weapons and equipment, German commanders were still seen to be outwardly confident that they could hold the centre together. Since the defeat at Moscow in late 1941 Army Group Centre had held the front lines and frequently fought with tenacity, repulsing repeated Russian attacks. Hitler, for one, believed if the Red Army were to unleash a large-scale summer offensive it would probably not be planned against the centre, for it had already proven to be well defended. In his view the Red Army would possibly attack northern Ukraine, offering Army Group Centre the best chance of survival. Not for one moment did Hitler nor his OKH commanders expect Army Group Centre to face the main Red Army drive.

Already German tactical intelligence, using radio interception and various reconnaissance units, had closely monitored enemy movements in the area and confirmed his opinion. Furthermore German intelligence had sent Hitler detailed reports in May 1944 that the main Red Army attack would be in the south, for they had detected large traffic movements. To substantiate their intelligence summary they had detected for sometime enemy units working on an extensive array of defences facing Army Group Centre positions. However, in spite of the positive reports on enemy concentration, by mid-1944 German intelligence-gathering was very restricted and somewhat unreliable. Not only was aerial reconnaissance limited due to massive Soviet air superiority, but on the ground, too, reconnaissance units were unable to collect extensive signal intelligence because of the strict Russian radio silence. But in May 1944 the Red Army had actually misled German intelligence regarding the presence and disposition of its forces. They had deceived Army Group Centre about the aims of the offensive and used a large-scale deception plan fooling the Germans into believing they were actually going to attack in the south, whereas the main objective was the centre.

Hitler now believed he was one step ahead of the Russians and in May ordered that vital equipment and resources be stripped from Army Group Centre to create a reserve to strike a pre-emptive blow in north Ukraine. As a result of this Army Group Centre lost most of its Panzers, a quarter of its self-propelled guns, and half its anti-tank capability as well as over a quarter of its heavy artillery.

With Army Group Centre stripped bare at the end of May, German intelligence began receiving disturbing reports that Russian armour was moving northwards. Days later there were strong indications that infantry divisions and artillery were concentrating opposite the army group's area. By the end of the first week of June four Soviet armies were detected opposite them.

On 19 June Army Group Centre Intelligence made a final report indicating that the Soviet offensive was now to be launched against the centre:

> The enemy attacks to be expected on Army Group Centre's sector – on Bobruisk, Mogilev, Orsha and possibly south-west of Vitebsk – will be of more than local character. All-in-all the scale of ground and air forces suggests that the aim is to bring about the collapse of Army Group Centre's salient by penetration on several sectors. On the other side the Red Army order of battle, so far as it is known or can be estimated, is not yet indicative of a deep objective.

Preparing the front line

As German intelligence began forewarning of the growing danger of a massive Russian offensive against Army Group Centre, commanders in the field realized that they had insufficient forces to defend their lines. Plans were immediately drawn up to withdraw and shorten the defensive positions in order to prevent the German forces from being encircled and then destroyed. General Ernst Busch, commander of Army Group Centre, asked Hitler if he could carry out a withdrawal in order to shorten the line and create reserves. The Führer, however, blatantly refused and told the General that the troops must improve their present positions and stand and fight. Hitler required every soldier on the front line to make an effective resistance in the face of overwhelming strength. Since March 1944, Hitler had been obsessed with his new 'Fester Platz' or 'Fortified Area' order (see Appendix II). These fortified areas were established in a number of main Russian towns and cities and were manned by strong German forces that were ordered to stem the Red Army onslaught by using various degrees of fanatical defence.

In Army Group Centre's area of operation the towns and cities of Bobruisk, Mogilev, Orsha and Vitebsk came under the Führer's 'Fortified Area' order. Although these areas were considered relatively strong, Hitler was determined to instil his defensive measures to the troops on the front lines as well. He believed that if he could hold back the Soviets, then this would prevent them using the central sector as a springboard into Poland. The war in the East could then be stretched out into a longer battle of attrition and stagnate once more for a fourth Russian winter.

Along the German front soldiers were slowly becoming aware of the imminent danger looming. As Army Group Centre intelligence monitored increased enemy activity German soldiers prepared their positions the best they could, with what limited materials and supplies they had at their disposal. Since late 1943 Army Group Centre had been relatively static and had managed during that time to build a large array of fortified defences. Defences were manned in special defensive regions and belts, anti-tank strong points, and an extensive network of engineer obstacles. The strength of the German defences varied considerably. Where it was expected that the main attack would take place, German commanders tried to concentrate the largest number of defenders on the narrowest frontages. In general, each division were able to build five or even six defensive belts to a depth of around 4 miles. Although these belts in many areas consisted of nothing more than lines of trenches with various tank obstacles, other sectors of the front were built into very impressive strongholds which included dozens of reinforced machine-gun and mortar pits. Each line of defence was heavily mined and consisted of many anti-tank strongpoints and a network of obstacles that were protected by extensive barbed wire barriers. Manning these lines were well dug-in soldiers that were armed with an assortment of weapons, which ranged from the standard Kar 98k bolt-action rifle, to captured Russian guns and highly effective Panzerfaust anti-tank rockets. The MG34 and MG42 machine guns were other weapons used extensively as a means of defence. Both types of machine gun were in ample supply in Russia during this period, but ammunition sometimes proved a problem. All along the front both the MG34 and MG42 were installed in series of machine gun pits and surrounded by anti-tank obstacles and lines of trenches with various assortments of Pak and artillery guns. The principal anti-tank weapon supplied to the divisions of Army Group Centre during this period was the 7.5cm Pak 40. On average some twenty-four of them were supplied to each division, which often helped supplement the diminishing numbers of the 8.8cm anti-aircraft gun. But in spite of the lethal arsenal of anti-tank weapons it was far from the amount needed to hold back the might of the Red Army. Like many parts of the front line, the Germans were overstretched, under-armed and undermanned. Consequently, soldiers were compelled to defend their position to the death knowing that they had limited stocks of weapons and shortages of ammunition. The lack of armoured support too was another deep concern for the German soldier and this brought about considerable apprehension. General Busch himself was under no elusion of the gargantuan task ahead. He had expressed his concerns openly with his field commanders and worries he had for his men carrying out the Führer's 'Fortified Area' order. General Hans Jordan scribbled in the Ninth Army war diary on 22 June 1944:

> Ninth Army stands on the eve of another great battle, unpredictable in extent and duration. One thing is certain: in the last few weeks the enemy has completed an assembly on the very greatest scale opposite the army, and the army is convinced that the assembly overshadows the concentration of forces off the north flank of Army Group North Ukraine … The army has felt bound to point out repeatedly that it considers the massing of strength on its front to constitute the preparation for this year's main Soviet offensive, which will have as its object the reconquest of Byelorussia. The army believes that, even under the present conditions, it would be possible to stop the enemy offensive, but not under the present directives which require an absolutely rigid defence … there can be no doubt … if a Soviet offensive breaks out the army will either have to go over to a mobile defence or see its front smashed …
>
> The army considers the orders establishing the 'fortified areas' particularly dangerous. The army, therefore, looks ahead to the coming battle with bitterness, knowing that it is bound by orders to tactical measures which it cannot in good conscience accept as correct and which in our own earlier victorious campaigns were the causes of the enemy defeats. One recalls the great breakthrough and encirclement battles in Poland and France. The commanding General and Chief of Staff presented these thoughts to the army group in numerous conferences, but there, apparently, the courage was lacking to carry them higher up, for no counter-arguments other than references to OKH orders were given. And that is the fundamental source of the anxiety with which the army views the future.

Opposing forces

On the eve of the Russian offensive Army Group Centre had a total of 34 infantry divisions, two Luftwaffe field divisions, two Panzergrenadier divisions, which included remnants of Panzergrenadier Division 'Feldherrnhalle', one Panzer division and seven security divisions. To the rear there were also a number of badly-depleted Hungarian divisions, which were regarded by the German commanders to be totally inadequate to fight. In total, the Germans boasted a force of some 400,000 troops with a further 400,000 of which were support units and non-combat positions. Although it was considered by the German High Command to be a significant force the length of the front in which the troops had to defend far outstretched their capabilities.

Opposing the German force were formidable Soviet forces totalling eight tank and mechanized corps, 118 rifle divisions, six cavalry divisions, 13 artillery divisions and 14 air defence divisions. There were some 1,700,000 soldiers and support personnel – more than double the strength of that of Army Group Centre.

All along the German front the Red Army continued building up its massive array of forces. Within days of the Soviet offensive they had allotted some 2,715 tanks and 1,355 assault-guns in order to exploit the enemy defensive positions and race ahead to secure key areas of ground.

On 22 June 1941 the German forces had gathered a massive force for the invasion of the Soviet Union consisting of over 3,000,000 troops, 139 divisions. These included 17 Panzer divisions, 10 motorized infantry divisions and one cavalry division. These forces were all divided into three great Army Groups: North, Centre and South. Army Group Centre contained 2nd Panzer Group consisting of five Panzer divisions (3, 4, 10, 17, and 18), and 3rd Panzer Group consisting of four Panzer divisions (7, 12, 19, 19, and 20), equipped with some 1,938 tanks. Here in this photograph is a long column of vehicles belonging to General Heinz Guderian`s 18th Panzer Division as it commences its long journey through the centre of Russia on 22 June 1941.

Army Group Centre's advance through Russia during the summer of 1941 was a rapid display of superiority. Everywhere there were scenes of complete devastation and carnage as German forces ripped through the Russian lines. In this photograph is an infantryman poised to throw an Stg24 stick hand grenade at a smoking building. This was the standard hand grenade used throughout the war and were commonly known by the men as the `potato masher`.

Troops try and relieve a vehicle that has become stuck along a typical muddy road. By October 1941, with still no sight of victory, the weather began to change for Army Group Centre with heavy downpours of rain turning previously dusty roads into a quagmire. The mud totally destroyed mobility and its effect had terrible problems for wheeled transport. In certain sectors of the front the mud was so bad that wheeled transport was either pushed to one side or else, as here, were pushed or towed through the worst stretches by tracked and semi-tracked vehicles.

German troops unable to progress any further occupy a Russian trench. By October 1941 the advance of Army Group Centre had gone from a glorious display of military might to a slow, pitiful slog eastward. To make matters worse since the advance on Moscow began at the end of September 1941, code-named `Operation Typhoon`, Army Group Centre had lost 35,000 men, 240 Panzers and over 800 other vehicles. Throughout the first half of October troops had been slogging up to their knees in mud and in some areas it brought the advance to a complete stop.

With a pair of binoculars a soldier scours the snow-covered terrain ahead during operations in Army Group Centre in December 1941. Outside Moscow to the west troops of Army Group Centre fought a desperate defensive action in freezing temperatures that reached 30 to 40 degrees below zero. Despair now gripped Army Group Centre as its battered and frostbitten forces stagnated in front of the Russian capital. Thankfully for the Germans the Red Army finally ran out of power because of the extreme weather, and was unable to achieve any deep penetration into the German lines. This had consequently saved Army Group Centre from complete destruction. Nevertheless, the battle had completely altered Army Group Centre from its glorious days in June 1941. From now on until it was finally forced further west two years later, it was to carry the scars of the battle of Moscow to its grave.

German troops using scissor binoculars in one of the many trenches that littered the frontlines of Army Group Centre in the summer of 1942. Following the terrible failure of Army Group Centre to capture Moscow, its forces managed to hold on to Rzhev, Vyazma, and Orel. Here the German front remained virtually unaltered and for months soldiers of Army Group Centre built permanent emplacements of logs and earth, which were reinforced by concrete guns and vast mine fields. In these positions the troops were relatively comfortable. In fact the situation was comparable to that of life on the Western Front in World War One.

A MG34 machine gun team move forward into action during some localised fighting with either Red Army troops or Partisans. For over twelve months Army Group Centre's front had solidified along a line of well-fortified positions. During this period they were confronted by an ever-growing number of attacks by huge bands of Partisan

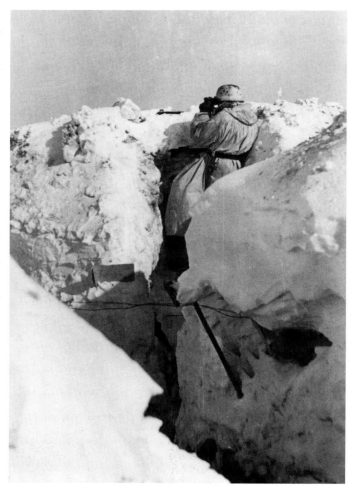

A German soldier operating on the front lines in Army Group Centre during the winter of 1943. Wearing a winter camouflage smock and a whitewashed steel helmet he can be seen looking through a pair 6 x 30 binoculars. The defensive lines built by the Germans in Russia during 1943 and 1944 was known as the East Wall, but little work was carried out because of huge shortages of materials needed for the Atlantic Wall. Some of the strongest defensives however were constructed in Army Group Centre.

Along part of Army Group Centre's East Wall is a German soldier looking through a pair of scissor binoculars in early 1944. It would be from these prepared defensive positions in Byelorussia that Army Group Centre would fight from. During the autumn of 1943 until June 1944 the front was relatively static enabling the Germans to carry out extensive field-fortification work.

Two smiling soldiers belonging to an unidentified German unit in Army Group Centre in March 1944. By this period of the war the quality of the infantry troops being drafted into Army Group Centre had steadily declined. With huge amounts of soldiers already dead and injured there were now thousands of Volksdeutsche, Alsatians, Poles and other ethnic minorities that were reluctantly pulled in to flood the dwindling ranks. Few were trained well and commanders became increasingly concerned that when the time came they would be unable to withstand strong Red Army attacks.

PART I

Operation Bagration Unleashed – 22–28 June 1944

Army Group Centre Attacked

Initially the Red Army offensive had actually been scheduled to commence on 19 June 1944, but had been postponed until 22nd due to supply problems and congestion caused by traffic.

During the evening of 21st long columns of Russian vehicles, guns and men finally moved forward towards their assembly areas. Thousands of Red Army troops joined other columns until the whole Russian front formed a continuous line of military might. The entire area had become a vast military encampment. Under trees beside roads stood hundreds of anti-aircraft and anti-tank guns, mines and other equipment. The soldiers were dwarfed by the immeasurable numbers of armoured vehicles parked in the woods and fields, where trucks, tanks, Katyusha rocket launchers and artillery pieces stood for mile after mile. In total there were some 1,700,000 Red Army soldiers and personnel preparing in earnest for the coming offensive. The front line strength amounted to some 1,250,000 troops. Most were impatient to end the months of inactivity and begin the battle upon which all their thoughts had been focused on for so long.

When night-time fell, units which were to form the first line of attack began drawing up towards the front line. Nearby the assault detachments moved up and waited with anxiety at their jumping off points. These units composed of sappers and infantry supported by heavy machine guns, mortars, and a number of tanks and self-propelled guns. Behind the assault detachments came advanced battalions, which were heavily supported by tank and self-propelled gun battalions.

As the Red Army completed its battle positions, there was a general feeling, not of elation at the thought of unleashing the greatest attack thus so far on the Eastern Front, but something more deeply ingrained, a firm belief to do its duty to the 'Motherland' and expel the invaders from its soil forever.

During the early hours of 22 June the morning was suddenly broken by the shouts of Russian gunnery officers giving the order for their men to begin a large artillery barrage. The artillery attack was in order to soften the German positions to allow company and battalion-sized infantry raids into the German defensive positions all along the front. In the Army Group Centre's War Diary it was noted:

> The major attack by the enemy northwest of Vitebsk has taken us by complete surprise. Until now our intelligence services had not indicated any type of enemy concentration of this size.

Almost immediately across vast parts of Army Group Centre the front line erupted in a wall of flame and smoke. Almost 22,000 guns and mortars and 2,000 Katyusha multiple rocket launchers poured fire and destruction onto the German defensive positions. Shell after shell thundered into the German strongpoints. In some sectors of the front German soldiers, fearing complete destruction, scrambled out of their trenches to save themselves from the rain of shells. In the northern sector of the German front near Sirotino the IX Corps took a massive pounding. As a precautionary measure and to help bolster the lines the 24th Infantry Division along with an assault gun brigade were quickly diverted under a rain of Katyusha and artillery fire and moved to the Third Panzer Army. In the area around Vitebsk a number of Red Army reconnaissance assaults were made, but the LIII Corps were able to repulse them without too much loss to their own men. Along the southern part of the line in Army Group Centre the defences seemed to hold much better and virtually all the Red Army attacks were blunted, preventing most penetrations.

Along the whole front the Russian artillery devoted the majority of its time to supporting the reconnaissance attacks and pulverising the German defensive positions and destroying areas deep in the German lines. From the air too came the Red Army Air force, which conducted around 1000 sorties against major troop concentrations and artillery positions. Initially though only about 150 sorties were flown due to early morning fog. However, later that day clearer weather gave way to more sorties.

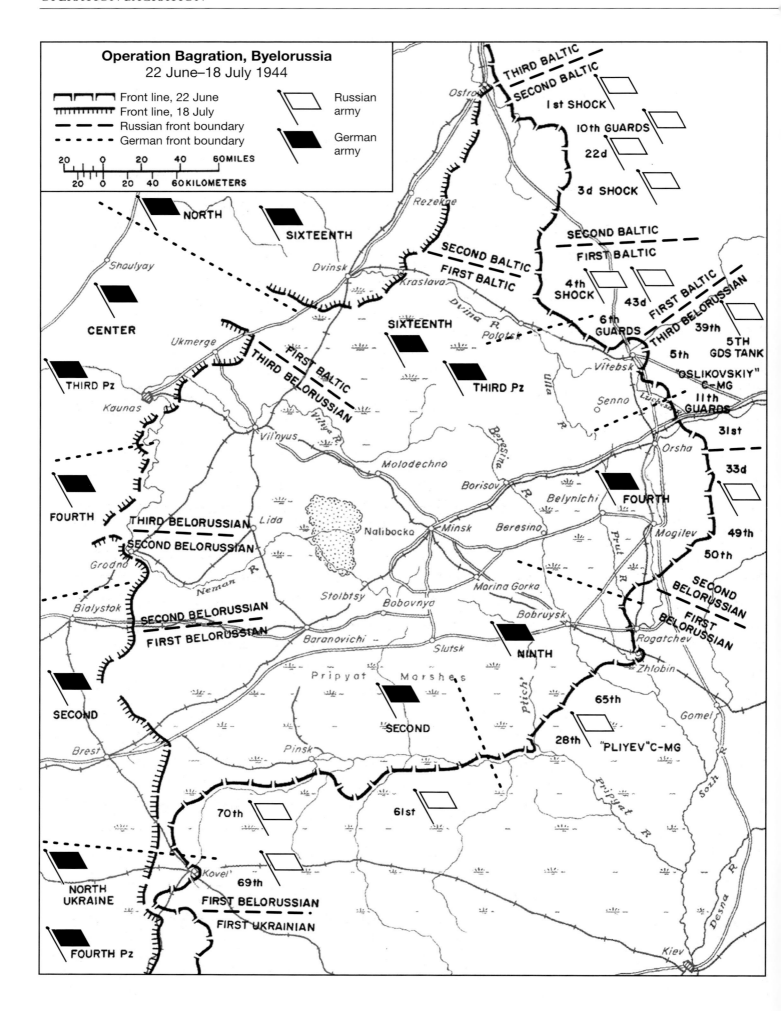

Operation Bagration, Byelorussia
22 June–18 July 1944

Front line, 22 June	
Front line, 18 July	
Russian front boundary	
German front boundary	

Russian army

German army

Whilst the Red Army Air Force dived and bombed, on the ground Russian artillery simultaneously pounded the German trench lines, to a depth of more than three miles in some places. The heavy artillery preparation lasted between one or two hours on average, but in some areas continued even longer. The attacking infantry were supported by a rolling barrage of artillery, and this continued with unabated ferocity until the troops had succeeded capturing the first two lines of the German defence.

By 0800 hours, three hours after the initial attacks, the Soviet artillery bombardment subsided. Much of the German front had held their positions against overwhelming odds, but the attack was not over. During the rest of the day the Red Army unleashed a huge attack of infantry and armoured vehicles against the German forward positions. All morning German defences endured ceaseless fire as the 1st Baltic and 3rd Belorussian Fronts attacked northwest and southeast of Vitebsk. The Third Panzer Army was engulfed in a sea of fire and explosions as it tried to hold its front line positions. Vitebsk was one of the major cities that were part of Hitler's 'fortified area' order, and German troops were duty-bound to hold it for as long as possible. Inside the fortified city of Vitebsk four German infantry divisions were given the awesome task of defending the city from the Russian onslaught. Just four months previous in February 1944 the Russians had been unsuccessful in trying to capture Vitebsk. Now, in June they were determined to capture the strategically important city at all costs.

The Red Army attack northwest of Vitebsk was a huge operation and had taken the Germans by complete surprise. Even the German intelligence services had observed such a large concentration of enemy troops in the area. Now the German force of the Third Panzer Army found themselves unexpectedly overwhelmed. The sudden speed and depth of the Russian attack was a brilliant display of all-arms coordination. For the first time in many months, the offensive had given each soldier an aura of invincibility that had not been enjoyed for sometime against Army Group Centre. As for the Germans, they were quite unprepared for the might of the Red Army. In some areas along the front units were simply brushed aside and totally annihilated. German survivors recalled that they had been caught off guard, lulled into a false sense of security by the previous weeks of inactivity along the front. Their commanders had assured them that the main attack would not fall in the centre, but the south. Now they were being attacked by the full brunt of the Red Army, and in some places were unable to mount an organised defence. In total confusion, hundreds of troops, disheartened and frightened, retreated in order to avoid the slaughter, whilst other more determined units remained ruthlessly defending their positions to the death.

Even during the initial stages of the offensive the Germans found that the Red Army were using new tactics. In other battles the Russians had attacked on a broad front with minimal artillery support. Now they had adopted the German method of attack by concentrating large numbers of infantry supported by heavy artillery and armour. From various observation posts dug along the front the Germans found that the Red Army attacked more heavily defended positions first before bringing up the assault groups. Once the assault groups made contact the armoured forces were then sent in to break through the lines.

By the early afternoon the Red Army had made considerable progress and battered the forward defensive positions of the Third Panzer Army. In fact, the fighting had been so severe that the IX Corps on the left flank of the Third Panzer Army had been pushed back four miles along a front of more than eight miles. Already the Germans were experiencing defensive problems in many areas and in spite of strong fortified positions, which were manned with Pak guns and lines of machine guns pits, the Red Army moved forward in their hundreds regardless of the cost in life to their own ranks. It soon became apparent to German commanders that both the 1st Baltic Front and 3rd Byelorussian Front might succeed in a gigantic pincer movement to cut-off the city of Vitebsk. Already there were no more reserves or reinforcements to help bolster the struggling Third Panzer Army. General Gollwitzer, commander of the LIII Corps, and who had been appointed as commandant of Vitebsk feared that his men would be annihilated if they held their defensive positions in front of the city. As the situation during the afternoon of 23rd deteriorated General Gollwitzer asked permission for his men to withdraw before they were surrounded. Later that day Hitler gave permission for the troops to withdraw, but only into the city as part of the 'Fortified Area' order.

By the end of the first day of the Russian attack the situation for Army Group Centre looked grim. All along the battered and blasted front German troops had tried in vain to hold their positions against overwhelming odds. For the Russians the offensive had progressed well and the city of Vitebsk was almost surrounded. Throughout the day Hitler had only permitted a limited withdrawal on certain sectors of the front. The Red Army, however, continued to exploit the German defences, especially those of the Third Panzer Army around Vitebsk.

In the 4th Army zone of operations the Russians were not as successful. The area along the main Moscow to Minsk highway was heavily defended with lines of fortified positions, mines and trenches belonging to General Traut's 78th Assault Division. Traut's men were the strongest German infantry formation in Byelorussia and boasted a heavy artillery support, which included some 31 StuG III assault-guns and 18 Nashorn self-propelled anti-tank guns. They were given the sole task of holding the highway supported by the well-equipped 25th Panzergrenadier Division, which covered Traut's southern flanks. In front of Traut's men and the 25th Panzergrenadier Division were special Red Army assault groups trained and equipped to smash through strong defensive positions. All morning and early afternoon the assault troops tried to breach Traut's defences troops, but the Germans were determined to hold at all costs and repelled the attackers using a variety of heavy and light artillery pieces supported by assault guns and groups armed with Panzerfaust rocket grenades.

Whilst the southern sector of Army Group Centre managed to hold large parts of its defences together, by the end of the day in the north German forces were crumbling against bitter opposition. Vitebsk was almost encircled and the Third Panzer Army was badly mauled. These were critical hours for the divisions of Army Group Centre. Over the next few days the once powerful German Army Group would strive to hold its positions using World War One tactics.

Decisive Battles

On 24 June the day opened as it had closed the day before with a series of successive attacks by the Red Army. The 1st Byelorussian Front was now embroiled in heavy fighting with the Ninth Army and had penetrated along its defensive positions north and south of the Beresina. The Fourth Army too had received a heavy battering, whilst in the Third Panzer Army sector, the Russians had successfully reached the town of Senno. Defences along the majority of Army Group Centre's front lines were either in turmoil or being ruptured by strong Soviet assault units. North of the smouldering city of Vitebsk the IX and VI Corps were being bled white from continuous fighting. Reserves had all but gone and those troops fighting to contain their meagre positions were at the end of their endurance. The 197th and 299th Infantry Divisions, which had tried to hold its lines around the city, were finally forced to withdraw along a 14-mile corridor. Without respite both infantry divisions fought their way northwest to avoid being totally destroyed. In the mayhem and confusion that swept the units the bulk of the wounded were reluctantly left behind. Many of the fleeing soldiers were left totally demoralised by the sheer weight of the Russian onslaught. In one sector of the front in the 299th Infantry Division the men had to suffer the Katyushas or 'Stalin Organs', as troops called them. These rocket machines with their distinctive shriek fired projectiles from 16-rail rocket launcher miles into the German lines. Although it was not a precision weapon, it was hardly necessary if 16 of them impacted an area about the size of four football pitches, dumping more than 300kg of explosives on the target. The terrifying noise they made was much feared by the Germans.

Slowly and systematically the Russians bulldozed their way through with German troops either fighting to the death, or saving themselves by escaping the impending slaughter by withdrawing to another makeshift position. By late morning on 24 June it was quite obvious to the commander of the Third Panzer Army, General Reinhardt that the Russians were attempting to encircle Vitebsk. During the early afternoon the Russians were converging on the city to the west and threatening to cut-off the LIII Corps. Almost immediately the 4th Luftwaffe Field Division was rushed southwest of Vitebsk in order to prepare a breakout operation. Reinhardt requested permission for the Luftwaffe division to commence operations to help relieve the LIII Corps, but yet again Hitler intervened and prevented the action. Instead two of the Corps own Luftwaffe divisions were used to prepare for two breakouts with two of the remaining infantry divisions. Late that evening as fighting intensified with even greater losses to the Germans around the city Hitler finally permitted the LIII Corps to withdraw from Vitebsk. However, the Führer ordered that General Hitter's 206th Infantry Division was to remain defending the city to the last man.

The following morning on 25 June, the first breakout attempt from the encircled city failed, in spite Hitler wanting Vitebsk held for another week. Fighting around the city had been a fierce contest of attrition, and although the Germans had showed great fortitude and determination, they were constantly hampered by the lack of weapons and manpower needed to sustain them on the battlefield. Consequently, the remaining troops holding out in the city were subjected to merciless ground and aerial bombardments. During the night of 25/26 June the situation had become hopeless for the beleaguered garrison. On 26 June, following a night of heavy artillery fire and constant infantry attacks, the Russian 39th Army finally succeeded in breaching a number of parts in the defences causing considerable casualties to the LIII Corps.

With the situation becoming graver by the hour General Gollwitzer, totally disobeying Hitler's orders, ordered a breakout of the LIII Corps. By the following morning on 27 June the Germans had broken out, but due to the ruthlessness of the Red Army attacks the Germans were forced into small battalion-sized units. Unabated fighting continued and losses were massive. Slowly and systematically the Germans were pulverised. Those troops fortunate enough to escape the impending slaughter immediately found themselves in open hostile countryside with lurking Russian partisans inflicting terrible casualties on them. As for the remaining troops of LIII Corps, some 5,000 were killed including three divisional commanders. The remaining 23,000 were captured. This included two divisional commanders taken prisoner, one of them was General Gollwitzer.

Elsewhere in Army Group Centre the fighting intensified as the Russians exploited the receding front lines by methodically reducing the German defences to a bombed and blasted rubble. The ferocity of the Soviet attacks was immense and without respite. After four long days of almost continuous battle the German soldier was exhausted and fighting for survival in a number of places. Hitler's insistence that his troops must fight from fixed positions without any tactical retreat had caused many units to become encircled by Red Army rifle divisions, leaving tank units to speed past unhindered and achieve deeper penetrations.

By 26 June the Red Army had achieved a number of successful encirclements. Around the city of Bobruysk for instance a total of 70,000 troops belonging to Ninth Army, were trapped in the city and to the east of it. Once again OKH had instructed that every soldier must hold every foot of ground forbidding any type of withdrawal. As a result of this stubborn order ten Red Army divisions closed in around the city of Bobruysk. The situation for the Ninth Army was critical, and the area around the city had become a vast killing ground. In just two days of fighting some 10,000 German troops had been killed around the city with a further 6,000 captured. Some soldiers, however, managed to claw their way through into the city only to find the situation just as dire.

On 27 June Bobruysk was completely cut-off and an understrength 12th Panzer Division was hastily moved in to try help relieve the siege. As the Red Army attempted to capture the city the commander of the XXXI Panzer Corps, General Hoffmeister, was given permission to attempt a breakout on the condition that one division hold the city under the command of General Hamann. It was not until 28 June that the breakout begun with waves of German troops slicing through a thin Russian line northwest of the city. Whilst the Germans tried to reach the lead elements of the Panzer Division along the Svisloch River, they were ruthlessly attacked. Although the breakout was regarded as a success with some 15,000 troops being saved from total annihilation, the men arrived along the banks of the river exhausted, demoralised and with virtually no weapons. As for the Russians they had left a trail of death and destruction. The city of Bobruysk was pounded into submission, and finally fell on 29 June.

Elsewhere in Army Group Centre the military situation was becoming increasingly desperate. Whilst many areas of the front simply cracked under the sheer weight of the Russian onslaught, a number of German units continued to demonstrate their ability to defend the most hazardous positions against well-prepared and highly superior enemy forces. German infantry divisions bitterly contested large areas of the countryside. Fighting was often savage, resulting in terrible casualties on both sides.

Despite the heavy resistance shown, the Germans still lacked the strength to contain the enemy. The Red Army continued to exploit both the northern and southern sectors of Army Group Centre, driving back or encircling the Germans as they went. On the Moscow to Minsk highway the Russians had fought doggedly against the stiff German defences of the 78th Assault Division. Although the 11th Guards Army had successfully penetrated the first line of German defences at a huge cost in casualties, the German division had withdrawn and prepared a second line of defence, east of Orekhovsk. By 25 June the 11th Guards Army finally overcame the second defensive belt and began an all out assault towards the city of Orsha. The 78th Assault Division, which had fought courageously since the beginning of the offensive, reluctantly withdrew and began moving southwest to help in the defence of the city. The next day on 26 June the 78th Assault Division had set up defensive positions in the northwestern suburbs of Orsha, but were soon under heavy attack from two Russian divisions. As the fighting intensified urgent requests were made to cancel the designation of Orsha as a 'Fortified Area', but this appeal was yet again denied. Instead, German troops in and around Orsha were compelled to fight to the death. As the battle continued to rage during the afternoon of 26th, Red Army forces began to encircle the city. Decimated German groups tried their best to hold, but many were forced to flee across open fields heavily infested with Russian soldiers. It was now only a matter of hours before Orsha would fall. One of the last troop trains to leave the city was quickly filled with wounded and hurriedly sent westward towards Minsk. As the locomotive steamed through the suburbs of the city it was unexpectedly attacked by a unit of T–34 tanks, blowing it off the rails and killing almost everyone on board. That night Orsha was finally captured.

By 28 June the situation for Army Group Centre was dismal. General Busch reported that the Ninth Army was significantly damaged with high losses. Fourth Army was retreating, and the Third Panzer Army was in a critical state with one corps left out of its original three. The entire front of Army Group Centre had been pierced in numerous places and although considerable numbers of troops were trying to hold their defensive positions, they were unable to avoid the encirclements. Nevertheless, Busch was determined to execute the Führer's Operations Order 8, which had demanded that all three armies immediately stop withdrawing and hold a new line due north and south of Beresino. Busch wasted no time and instructed the three armies to halt, but the damage to them was far beyond repair.

During the day Hitler decided to finally replace Busch with Field Marshal Model in order to instil new vigour and restore determination into Army Group Centre. The change in command pleased many of the commanders in the Army Group. Many of them had been bitter over the developments, which had resulted in the way that Army

Group Centre had been led. General Nikolaus Vormann for one, who had replaced General Jordan as Commander in General, received the news with 'satisfaction and renewed confidence'. Many of the commanders in the field including the soldiers looked upon Model as the Führer's troubleshooter. He had been the commander that had first introduced in early 1944 the 'Shield and Sword' policy on the Eastern Front, which stated that retreats were intolerable, unless they paved the way for a counterstroke later. Out on the battlefield Model was not only energetic, courageous and innovative, but was friendly and popular with his enlisted men. Now commander of Army Group Centre he was given the awesome task of trying to minimize the extent of the disaster. With twenty-eight of its thirty-seven divisions destroyed or surrounded, Model was called upon to rescue the remnants and stabilize the front from complete annihilation.

During the last few days before Operation Bagration was unleashed a Pak team can be seen going through firing procedures whilst under the command of their officer. Although German artillery was generally overwhelmed by the intensity of the Russian arsenal, it did provide the core of the defensive success of the German Army during the last year of the war. The Pak gun was one weapon that proved its worth in combat and ensured that troops were able to counter the massive array of Russian armour with some success.

A mortar crew fire an 8cm GrW 34 medium mortar during the early phase of the Russian attack. This particular weapon remained the standard German infantry mortar throughout the war. Its combined firepower with excellent mobility provided excellent indirect fire support at short range and was used extensively by the German Army in defence in the summer of 1944.

StuG III`s being loaded onboard flatbed railway cars destined for Army Group Centre. These vehicles would soon be regarded as the backbone of the German armour in Army Group Centre and would become fiercely embroiled in heavy fighting. Between late May and 22 June 1944 hundreds of railroads carloads of troops, supplies, ammunition and armour were dispatched to the Eastern Front to help bolster Army Group Centre.

One of the extensive trenches dug along the front line of Army Group Centre during the first half of 1944. From his trench a German soldier can be seen scouring the terrain ahead using a pair of binoculars. Although the German defensive positions seemed quite impressive, given the length of the front to be defended, German infantry divisions were stretched beyond their capabilities.

A German soldier watches as a battery of Nebelwerfers are fired toward Russian positions. Although designed primarily as an anti-personnel weapon, these rockets proved lethal against enemy positions. After the crew had loaded and aimed the launcher, they would take cover a few feet away and then fire the weapon by an electric wire. As in this photograph after firing a long streak of smoke could be seen from far away, making the Nebelwerfer an excellent target for counter-artillery fire. It was therefore necessary to relocate the Nebelwerfer as soon as possible after firing.

A photograph of a 15cm Nebelwerfer 41, which fired a range of 15cm spin-stabilised rockets. Fully loaded this weapon fired six 34kg (74.8lb) Wurfgrenate 41 rockets to a maximum range of 6900m (7553yds). It took roughly 10 seconds to fire a full salvo, but because the launcher had to be manually loaded it could fire only three salvoes in five minutes. Although this earlier model was not used extensively on the Eastern Front in 1944, it was still seen in action with the Nebeltruppen.

Nebeltruppen pose for the camera with their 15cm Nebelwerfer 41. Although the organisational establishment varied, the standard battalion organisation consisted of four batteries of six 15cm Nebelwerfers, which amounted to a total of 24 launchers and 144 barrels. This was considered more than enough firepower to seriously hinder enemy troop concentrations. The Nebelwerfer 41 was replaced with a slightly lighter version called the Nebelwerfer 42, which had five barrels instead of the six. This newer model was equipped with removable internal rails in the tubes to allow for the use of the 15cm rocket. Both types were towed pieces which were mounted on the modified carriages of a light pre-war anti-tank gun.

A Luftwaffe mortar unit near the city of Vitebsk during the early stages of Bagration. From a well-prepared pit the crew get ready to fire a mortar during heavy exchanges of fire with advancing Soviet forces. During the initial stages of the Russian summer offensive Soviet forces swept south of Vitebsk and encircled it. Both the 4th and 6th Luftwaffe Field Divisions, which were part of LIII Army Corps, were given the primary mission of holding the southern and eastern parts of the city at all costs. However, after being systematically ground down in a battle of attrition for three days both Luftwaffe field divisions collapsed after a poorly co-ordinated breakout from the city.

Two soldiers take cover inside a trench. The quality of the German soldier in the summer of 1944 had steadily declined, due to the massive casualties inflicted on them. Since 1943 there had been a steady arrival of ethnic Germans from Eastern Europe being drafted into the ranks of Army Group Centre. Although they appeared willing to fight they were unable to withstand determined Russian attacks, which sometimes meant that they had to endure bitter defensive actions for long periods of time.

A Luftwaffe flak gunner with his flak gun during the first days of Bagration. As with all flak guns they were primarily designed to deliver a barrage of exploding shells against enemy aircraft. The effectiveness of such flak fire generally required firing literally thousands of rounds of ammunition in order to prevent the enemy aircraft from completing their mission successfully. During the 1944 summer offensive both the 2cm and 3.7cm flak gun was also used in a ground role against advancing Russian units.

On the front lines of Army Group Centre in 1944. This scene is typical of the devastation left after prolonged heavy Russian bombardment. Literally hundreds of soldiers were killed leaving the area comparable to that of conditions fought during the First World War.

German troops appear to be under fire and keep low to the ground. A medical aid man treats a wounded soldier's leg. For the opening of the Russian summer offensive the Red Army launched massive artillery strikes with the sole objective of smashing the German positions and keeping the remnants pinned down for hours on end under a hurricane of fire.

German horse-drawn transport comes under a heavy artillery attack on 23 June 1944. These Russian bombardments helped saturate the objectives and thus pave the way for the main Red Army advance. For the German soldier that had to endure the savage attacks it was described as being an intensity and destructiveness never seen during the war on the Eastern Front. The Russian artillery preparation was supposed to have been accompanied by heavy aerial attacks, but early morning fog and smoke for the battlefield restricted the air raids in a number of places. However, much of the emphasis was on the preliminary ground attack and this was very successful.

One of the many defensive belts constructed along the front in Army Group Centre. These defensive positions, apart from being heavily mined and protected by extensive barbed wire entanglements, anti-tank barriers, Pak and Flak gun positions, were also reinforced with MG34 and MG42 machine guns. Here in this photograph a machine gunner can be seen armed with his MG42 machine gun.

A StuG III moves across open ground during the initial stages of Bagration. By 1944 the StuG III had become an extremely common assault gun, especially on the Eastern Front. The StuG had been slowly absorbed into Panzer units, Panzer and Panzergrenadier divisions of the Wehrmacht and Waffen-SS. However, in spite of the assault guns numerous advantages, equipping some of the Panzer units did not blend well with the nature of the Panzer. Yet, because of the lack of tanks in the dwindling ranks of the Panzer divisions, the StuG III was used alongside the Panzer until the war ended.

Two StuG III assault guns have halted inside one of the many decimated villages along the front line. The StuG III provided its worth as invaluable anti-tank weapon. In a number of last-ditch battles it continued to show its true capabilities as a tank killer. But despite its proven tank-killing potential and its service on the battlefield, the StuG III gradually deprived the infantry of the vital fire support for which the assault gun was originally built, in order to supplement the massive losses of Panzers.

A blurred photograph showing Nebeltruppen pulling a Nebelwerfer to a new firing position. Although the Nebelwerfer were regarded as a highly effective weapon, when the rockets were fired it left a long trail of smoke making it detectable from a relatively long distance away. It was therefore imperative that once the troops fired the Nebelwerfer they immediately relocated to another position before resuming action again.

A MG34 machine gun team pass a knocked out T-34 tank. The Red Army enjoyed substantial numerical superiority against the Germans in everything including armoured vehicles. During the early phase of Bagration the Russians had some 2,715 tanks and 1,355 assault guns, which was roughly six times the amount Army Group Centre could field. The majority of the Russian tanks used for the offensive were the T-34/85.

A halftrack tows a 15cm artillery piece to the front. Although the 15cm gun was used on the front lines of Army Group Centre, crews found that they were cumbersome and very heavy, especially when they needed to be quickly dismantled and moved to another sector of the front. During Bagration the battle moved so rapidly that crews were often compelled to leave their heavy artillery behind, regularly destroying them before they left.

The crew of a PzKpfw IV have halted on a road. The vehicle has received a summer-camouflaged scheme and has intact side skirts. There were only a handful of PzKpfw IV`s in Army Group Centre. But against the T-34 tank it effectively demonstrated its superiority on the battlefield and won a number of defensive battles alongside the Tiger and Panther.

The T-34 tank was the most popular armoured vehicle in the Red Army. Here in this photograph one of the many T-34 tanks used against Army Group Centre has been knocked out of action and has thrown a track. During the initial stage of the offensive Russian armour together with mechanised and cavalry units exploited the German front lines and penetrated the defensive belt.

A flak gun mounted on the back of an artillery tractor moves forward into action towing an ammunition trailer. By 1944 mechanised formations had become well equipped with flak guns and these were used extensively on the battlefield in both offensive and defensive actions. The hinged sides and rear railings of the vehicle have been removed to allow extra space onboard the halftrack and to provide a wider firing platform for the gunners.

A SdKfz 253 halftrack crosses a wooden bridge. This particular vehicle is being used as a light armoured personnel carrier or for reconnaissance duties. Reconnaissance duties were probably the most dangerous duties to undertake on the battlefield. Under cover they had to probe forward, survey enemy positions until they encountered enemy fire and then return with vital information, specifically the location of the enemy.

Two StuG III's move through a village. The StuG III was the most common German armoured vehicle in Army Group Centre and these assault guns provided much needed fire-support to the infantry divisions. They were also very useful for anti-tank defence. In total there were some 480 StuG III infantry assault guns during the opening phase of the Russian offensive. The heaviest concentration of armour was found in the Fourth Army, which was defending the tactically important city of Orsha.

An interesting photograph showing a unit of SdKfz 251 halftrack in action. These halftracks were often seen in the thick of battle, debussing their troops and mopping up the enemy before returning to be moved to another battle line. The SdKfz 251 was the most popular vehicle used by the Panzergrenadiers and was frequently seen in battle, moving alongside tanks and providing the latter with valuable support.

A tracked vehicle towing a well camouflaged Pak gun. Despite the ever-increasing demand on anti-tank guns, there were never enough anti-tank guns to protect the German divisions that were exposed almost daily to the full might of the Red Army. Nonetheless, the Germans continued to fight on with what they had at their disposal and displayed all the skill and élan that made them one of the best fighting formations in the world.

Two SdKfz 7 flak halftracks have their gun barrels elevated towards the sky after the crews having evidently detected Soviet aircraft. During Bagration the Russians had overwhelming advantage in airpower, and this was more effective due to the almost complete lack of German fighters to protect Army Group Centre. In total the Russians had 21 fighter divisions, 14 strike divisions, 8 bomber divisions, 16 strategic bomber divisions, 6 night bomber divisions and 179 reconnaissance aircraft. In total the Red Army Air force had 5,327 combat aircraft including 1,007 bombers.

Grenadiers withdraw through a destroyed town. During the initial shelling of the German trench lines, the Russians concentrated their fire to a depth of 3 or 4 miles. This was undertaken in order to crush the forward German positions so that it would allow infantry and armour to pour through the gaps.

Troops loading barrels of fuel onboard a Nashorn. In addition to the Panzers and assault guns there a few hundred tank destroyers, including a number of Nashorns. Although this particular tank destroyer had inadequate armour protection, it was armed with very powerful long-barrelled 8.8cm anti-tank gun. There was limited space inside the fighting compartment, which allowed storage for only 24 to 40 rounds. Nashorn crews travelled in open-top fighting compartments, but were protected against the harsh weather conditions by canvas covers. The armoured vehicle lacked a machine gun in the hull, but a single MG34 or MG42 was carried inside the fighting compartment for local defence.

A SdKfz 251/10 halftrack and another armoured vehicle scour the sky for Soviet aircraft. The halftrack is armed with a 3.7cm PaK36 flak gun. Soviet aircraft were a constant hindrance to German troop movement and hampered all efforts of regaining any long-term defence. With the absence of the Luftwaffe, Russian aircraft could more or less roam at will, causing unprecedented damage on troop concentration and supply columns.

During a lull in the battle somewhere along the front the crew of an SdKfz 251 have time to relax and hang some of their washed clothing to dry between two trees. From the very early years of the war the halftrack had transformed the fighting quality of the armoured divisions. They not only carried the infantry alongside the advancing Panzers, but also brought machine guns, mortars, boxes of ammunition and supplies. They also towed Pak guns and light flak guns, howitzers and pontoon-bridge sections to the forefront of the battle. Predominantly the halftrack was the preferred vehicle for carrying infantry and Panzergrenadiers into battle.

A Panther in action inside a village during the initial stage of the offensive. All along the front the Red Army rapidly moved forward in a series of heavy penetrating strikes taking advantage of their superior manpower and huge tank forces. In order to help combat these deep penetrations the Germans organised the Panthers into mobile counter-attack units. These units smashed through the flanks of any Soviet attacks and inflicted heavy losses. But what thwarted the Panther crews was the fact they did not have enough Panthers to counter the sheer weight of the Soviet tank forces.

An 8.8cm flak gun in action. The 8.8cm flak gun was perhaps the most famous German artillery gun during World War Two. With the considerably heavier and more lethal Soviet armour the gun was specifically designed for a dual-purpose role, possessing a very potent anti-tank capability as well. In many parts of the front in Army Group Centre many units had barely enough Panzers to oppose the Russian armour and called upon the flak battalions to try and halt the Red Army's relentless advance.

Red Army troops belonging to an unidentified rifle unit pass a destroyed Russian tank. Russian rifle divisions were normally smaller than German divisions, averaging around 3000 – 4000 troops. However, before Bagration was launched Russian commanders strove to increase this number to nearly 6,000 soldiers.

A T-34 tank moves along a dusty road bound for the German lines. The T-34 was built in vast quantities and while it was not a perfect machine, it perhaps had the best fighting qualities in a tank during the war on the Eastern Front. During Bagration the T-34 was the most common tank used.

Russian troops move into action after heavy artillery wrenches open a part of the German front line. The Red Army enjoyed massive superiority over the Germans in artillery. In total they had a staggering 10,563 artillery pieces, which were greater than 7.6cm in calibre, and some 2,306 multiple rocket launchers. There were an additional 4,000 anti-tank guns and 11,514 mortars.

A StuG III can be seen halted on the left of the photograph with one of the crewmembers watching a SdKfz 251 halftrack moving a long a dusty road. The most powerful German infantry division in Army Group Centre was the 78th Assault Division. Not only did the division have heavier artillery support, but boasted 31 StuG III assault guns and 18 Nashorn self-propelled anti-tank guns.

Russian gunners return fire with a 45mm Model 1932 L/46 gun in support of advancing Soviet troops. Although Russian infantry tactics generally caused high casualties the tactic frequently unbalanced the enemy and drove them from their defensive positions in chaotic disorder.

Two soldiers holding mines move forward into action near city of Vitebsk. Within hours of the Russian offensive Red Army forces were already making substantial inroads into the German defences and reports soon confirmed that the 1st Baltic Front and 3rd Byelorussian Front would succeed in a combined pincer movement around Vitebsk.

Moving along a road a Tiger passes a knocked-out Russian tank. The total strength of Tigers in Army Group Centre amounted to some 29, and these were mainly found in the 505th Heavy Tank Battalion. This heavy tank battalion was one of the best-known armoured formations that saw action during the offensive where it first encountered heavy fighting near the town of Borisov with the 5th Panzer Division.

A halftrack taking cover behind some trees during a lull in the battle. This photograph was taken in the 20th Panzer Divisions area of operations. By 26 June 1944 units of the 20th Panzer Division were ordered to disengage south of Bobruisk and move to block the southwestern approaches to the city. However, soon the 20th Panzer Division's situation rapidly began to deteriorate and it was compelled to pull out before it was totally annihilated.

Making its debut in Russia for the first time is an 8.8cm Pak gun seen here in action. This new anti-tank gun was a very powerful and deadly weapon and it was soon regarded by friends and foe alike to be the finest anti-tank gun ever produced during the war. But production was still very limited and consequently there were never enough 8.8cm guns to protect every German infantry unit.

A StuG III assault gun moves across open ground. For the German infantry the large deployment of assault guns and self-propelled guns in Army Group Centre provided indispensable firepower that they desperately needed in order to combat the sheer weight of the Soviet tank force.

A knocked-out German eight-wheeled vehicle can be seen inside a burning town. All over Army Group Centre scenes of destruction appeared everywhere as the Red Army rapidly sliced its way through German defensive positions and began encircling towns and cites that were heavily defended by German troops.

The crew of a StuG III preparing their assault gun for further action. In spite of the strength of the Red Army the StuG III continued to prove a valuable support and scored a number of successes during engagements throughout the offensive.

During the battle of Vitebsk a German Pak crew can be seen in the thick of battle trying to defend their positions to the death. By 24 June Red Army forces encircled Vitebsk with parts of the 206th Infantry Division trapped inside. For almost two days the Russian Air Force pounded the city. During the evening of 26 June the German situation had become so desperate that by the following day units began trying to escape from the city. By the time the city fell few German troops had escaped and reached their lines. In total some 20,000 German troops had been killed during the battle and 10,000 captured. It had been a complete disaster for the Germans.

A mortar crew in action trying in vain to defend its position. After more than four days of constant fighting Hitler`s refusal to permit his forces to tactically withdraw and contain them in fixed defensive positions inevitably led Red Army rifle divisions to encircle and destroy them with relative ease.

A halftrack has been equipped with a 3.7cm flak gun and can be seen hidden in undergrowth in order to afford some protection from enemy observation. These mobile flak guns were used extensively in Army Group Centre and helped contain the Red Army during a number of heavy engagements.

During the defence of Orsha a Luftwaffe Flak crew pose for the camera during a lull in the fighting. German troops were ordered to defend Orsha to the grim death, but as it looked increasingly like the city would fall units were ordered to withdraw.

Another photograph of the same Luftwaffe flak position, but this time showing the young gunner looking through his optical sight. The defence of Orsha was bitterly contested by the 78th Assault Division, but they had neither the manpower nor weaponry to hold back the enemy. Consequently, on the night of 26–27 June after heavy combined fighting by the 11th Guards Army and 31st Army, the city was captured.

Soldiers of the 6th Luftwaffe Field Division in a defensive position near the city of Vitebsk. The 6th Luftwaffe Field Division fought in the north of Army Group Centre and was part of the Third Panzer Army. The initial Russian attack in their sector just east of Vitebsk had come as a complete surprise and within days was being driven west whilst being endlessly bombed and blasted by heavy aerial and ground attacks.

A German soldier in one of the many defensive positions dug along the front lines of Army Group Centre. The Red Army advance was so swift that frequently these German positions were abandoned and then occupied by Russian troops, enabling the latter to secure their positions more rigidly.

A Russian T-34 tank has been knocked out of action near to the Orsha highway. Dead horses and various supplies from a horse-drawn wagon are scattered in the field. It was along the Orsha highway that the Red Army attempted to breakthrough the heavily defended positions of the 78th Assault Division.

Nebeltruppen move their Nebelwerfer out from a forest in order to prepare it for firing against advancing Russian units. The Nebelwerfer can clearly be seen fitted onto a converted 3.7cm Pak carriage. During Bagration the Nebelwerfer was found to be a very effective weapon when used against infantry. It fired a pattern of six projectiles that screamed into the air, creating a terrifying noise.

A 15cm sFH 18/1 Fgst auf Gschw III/IV Hummel SP gun of unidentified unit, Eastern Front, Summer 1944. Hummels generally served with Panzer Artillery Regiments within Panzer Divisions. (Wydawnictwo Militaria)

Lend-lease Valentine tanks from the Russian 5th Tank Army, Byelorussia, June 1944. (Wydawnictwo Militaria)

German assault guns on Byelorussia in June 1944. (Wydawnictwo Militaria)

StuG 40 Ausf G from the 906 StuG
Battalion, Byelorussia, June 1944.
(Wydawnictwo Militaria)

Hummel from 73rd Panzer Artillery
Regt, 4th Panzer Division, June 1944.
(Wydawnictwo Militaria)

PART II

Fighting for Survival – 29 June–6 July 1944

Army Group Centre Retreats

When Field Marshal Model took command of Army Group Centre on 28 June he quickly decided how he was going to deal with the difficult situation. With the massive holes that had been punched in many places along the German front lines he could not hope for any appreciable length of time to slow down the mighty Red Army drive. What made the situation even more difficult was the fact that he did not have any form of communication with the Fourth Army that was fighting west of Minsk, or its commander, General Tippelskirch. Radio communications too with the Ninth Army, which was encircled in Bobruisk, were constantly failing and he could not get a clear picture of the events that were dramatically unfolding. The only reliable source of information that he could obtain was from the Third Panzer Army.

The most important task Model had to undertake was to rescue both the Fourth and Ninth armies. Due to no communications with either army the Field Marshal had to produce a rough assessment, which consequently limited the success of the operation. In view of the dire circumstances that Army Group Centre faced, Model was more than aware that the fate of these divisions trapped was probably already sealed. Although these were critical days he was still determined to try and avert the situation by opening up the pockets, pulling the troops out and withdrawing them back to build new defensive lines.

Out on the battlefield the condition of the troops varied considerably. Whilst some areas of the front were demoralised often without sufficient weapons, others parts were heavily defended with a formidable force. One such powerful formation was the 5th Panzer Division. This was sent direct from the Ukraine by rail to help block the advancing Russian forces on the Moscow-Minsk highway. It was reinforced with 55 Pz Kpfw IV's, 70 Panthers, and 29 Tiger Is belonging to the 505th Heavy Tank Battalion. The main objective of the 505th was to hold the Berezina river line and allow withdrawing units of the Fourth Army to retreat to safety. When the 5th Panzer Division arrived there was utter confusion in the area. Littered along the roads going west over the Berezina bridges there were countless numbers of abandoned equipment and burning vehicles. They found that large numbers of troops were demoralised, exhausted and often without weapons. Stocks of supplies were almost non-existent and many of them had not eaten in days.

It was not until the night of 28/29 June that the 5th Panzer Division made first contact with the Third Byelorussian Front. The fighting raged all night. Following almost twenty-four hours of bitter and bloody combat, German infantry were permitted to fallback into the town of Borisov, while armour of the 5th Panzer Division held parts of the line. For the next day or so the Germans attempted to hold their meagre positions, but by 30 June the Red Army had pierced the Berezina in a number of places and there were no more mobile reserves to counter-attack. As a consequence the 3rd Guards Tank Corps together with the 5th Guards Rifle Division began encircling Borisov. What followed was a bitter battle to break into the city. All over Borisov there were roadblocks and crude defence barriers as hard-pressed German troops desperately tried to hold their positions before the city. When Red Army troops finally broke into the city vicious street battles erupted. For a number of hours a motley assorted collection of German soldiers engaged in a bitter battle, trying in varying degrees of bravery to repulse the never-ending stream of Russian troops. However, as casualties drastically rose the survivors retreated from the city during the night of 30 June, leaving the Russians to capture Borisov.

Signs of disintegration now plagued every sector of the front. By 1 July the situation in many areas of Army Group Centre was almost impossible to control. Although a number of sectors held their ground large parts of the front was on the point of collapse. In less than a week the First Byelorussian Front had killed 50,000 German troops and captured some 20,000. They had destroyed or captured over 2,500 artillery pieces, and more than 350 armoured vehicles. Both the Ninth and Fourth Armies were now trapped in a huge pincer movement and were being slowly and systematically bled to death on the battlefield. For hours German troops were subjected to merciless low-level Soviet fighters and blasted by artillery. In a desperate attempt to survive troops hastily dug trenches to try and protect themselves from the incessant shelling.

With the slow collapse of the Fourth and Ninth Armies came the worrying prospect that the city of Minsk would soon fall. Minsk was another city under Hitler's 'Fortified Area' order. However, it was only defended by 1,800 under-equipped soldiers. To bolster this small force were around 15,000 stragglers that had hurriedly withdrawn into the city to avoid being destroyed, but these were mainly unarmed, exhausted and demoralised soldiers. For the defence of Minsk a number of disjointed units held the approaches to the city whilst some 12,000 rear-echelon staff from Army Group Centre's headquarters prepared to evacuate west, along with several thousand wounded. In order to keep open the main railways lines for evacuation to the north of the city the 5th Panzer Division concentrated its main armour consisting of the 505th Heavy Tank Battalion and 31st Panzer Regiment.

The following day on 2 July Red Army forces begun storming into the eastern suburbs of Minsk supported by two batteries of self-propelled guns. The heavy exchanges of firing then spilled over into intense street fighting between Russian soldiers and teams of German troops armed with Panzerfaust anti-tank rocket launchers. The situation inside the city became increasingly disorganized for the Germans. Communication networks no longer existed and orders were now issued by word of mouth. The chaos was so bad that officers arriving to take over units soon discovered nothing to take over, because their commands had already been captured or annihilated. In most areas well-armed soldiers were left leaderless, and did not know exactly where they were fighting or who was fighting on their flanks. By early morning of 3 July with the evacuation of the city complete the last remaining units that had been defending east of Minsk were trapped, captured, or destroyed. Others demoralized groups of soldiers broke and ran trying to escape westward. The few remaining soldiers that stood resolute against the Soviets were now steadily driven back into the centre of Minsk. In these vast wastelands what had once been broad roads and streets were now pitted paths that criss-crossed through mountains of rubble. This was where the last German troops held out in defence of Minsk until forward units of the 1st Guards Tank Corps of the First Byelorussian Front finally liberated the city.

With the loss of Minsk the 5th Panzer Division was ordered to keep open a corridor for withdrawing forces that were moving northwest through Molodechno. Ferocious fighting continued throughout the day as units of the 5th Panzer Division and the 13th Panzergrenadier Regiment clashed with the 3rd Guards Cavalry Corps and 3rd Guards Mechanised Corps. The 505th Heavy Tank Battalion, which bore the burnt of many of the attacks, scored considerably well against the advancing Russian armour. In just six days of combat it had successfully knocked out 295 Soviet tanks of which 128 were destroyed by the Tiger tanks. Fighting though in the area was very confusing and German communication between the various commands was repeatedly lost, making the situation much worse. German soldiers that were embroiled in heavy contact with the enemy for long periods often found that their rear positions had already been evacuated. As a result the troops were regularly exposed to heavier fire without support, and in many circumstances were quickly encircled and then destroyed.

For Army Group Centre the main objective had been the same as it had been during the beginning of the Russian offensive, to try and build new lines of defences and stem the Russian onslaught, or at least slow it down. After the fall of Minsk the main priority for the Germans was to build a strong defensive belt along the main railway line near Vilnius, and to assist the Third Panzer Army and Fourth Army that were fighting for survival trying to escape from the claws of the Russian drive. The 5th Panzer Division was given yet another task in delaying the Red Army for as long as possible, despite its units being significantly worn down and totally exhausted. In opposition to very high odds of almost twenty-times its strength the remaining Tigers and Panthers supported by well-armed grenadiers continued with unabated ferocity to fight with courage and zeal. As desperation gripped the battered and bruised front lines troops became much more reliant on both the Tiger and Panther for defence. Since 1942 the Tiger had dominated the battlefield on the Eastern Front, and although by 1944 there were never enough available in sufficient numbers in the defensive battles, they still played a key role. Again and again these armoured monsters demonstrated their awesome killing power playing a prominent position in Army Group Centre's defence against numerically superior Soviet armoured forces. But with the tide turned against the German Army they were overstretched and slowly destroyed. Over the next few days the division's formidable tank strength was reduced from its original 70 Panthers, 55 PzKpfw IVs and 20 Tigers of the 505th Heavy Tank Battalion to just 12 Panthers, 6 Pz Kpfw IVs and two or three Tigers. Luckily for the tank crews a number of the knocked-out Panzers could be successfully salvaged from the battlefield by one of the independent maintenance companies and taken to a nearby workshop to be repaired, in order for them to fight another day.

Disintegration of Army Group Centre

By 4 July the military situation of Army Group Centre was calamitous and it was fast becoming clear, even to the least knowledgeable German soldier, how rapidly their army was diminishing. The absence of communications too made it impossible for the Germans to access the full extent of disintegration. There seemed no stopping the tide of the Russian advance, and as they remorselessly pushed forward German formations became increasingly confused and entangled in bitter bloody fighting. In some areas the fighting was so fierce that is was virtually impossible to distinguish between friend or foe. Engagements like this had been fought scores of times on the Eastern Front, but many believed never with such ferocity. Mercy was often neither offered nor given by both sides during these confrontations. Almost continuously Soviet pressure was maintained, whilst German commanders strove desperately to stabilise the situation. Whilst some areas still held fanatically a general breakdown began to sweep the lines. German soldiers were completely stunned by the weight of the blow that had hit Army Group Centre. After more than ten days fighting the battlefield had become wrought with death and destruction. Although the German soldier was generally determined as ever to fight, they were constantly being isolated and trapped by superior numbers of enemy infantry. Areas that still remained in German hands were slowly reduced to a few shrinking pockets of resistance.

As the situation deteriorated further Field Marshal Model could do nothing to avert the looming catastrophe. His ultimate concern now was the severe lack of troops and equipment needed to hold new lines of defence. Because the Red Army had torn open the front, he had nothing in which to slow down the advance. Since taking command of Army Group Centre Model had repeatedly requested for reinforcements, but hardly any arrived. On 4 July he received a combat situation report outlining that his depleted and worn-out forces consisting of only eight formations had to fight on a 280-mile wide front against some 42 enemy tank brigades, 16 motorized infantry brigades, six cavalry divisions and no less than 116 rifle divisions. With the grave situation increasingly worsening by the hour OKH finally decided to dispatch an additional division from Army Group North to Dvinsk. Hitler himself very concerned over the prospect of Army Group Centre completely collapsing ordered that Army Group North was to establish contact with the left flank of the Third Panzer Army. Although the plan seemed like it would stabilise the northern part of Army Group Centre, Model remarked that only swift action could bring about acceptable and long-lasting results to the front.

In the south of Army Group Centre the problems were just as bad with large areas of troop concentrations battered to the point of where they were paralysed. Despite the fact that new defensive lines were constructed troop strength and the lack of weapons were so depleted that nothing could be done to prevent many units becoming encircled and then annihilated. Although there were many appeals for reinforcements to the frontal sectors, Hitler would not allow the deployment of any new troops from Army Group North Ukraine, due to the expected enemy attack in that area. This meant that promised troop units never arrived.

All over Army Group Centre various formations that were not encircled or tied down in bitter fighting withdrew, all attempting to get through to the main German lines that were moving westward. Morale was reported to be terribly low among many of the troops. Fear of falling into Russian hands, particularly those of partisans, was a constant worry. Soldiers frequently came across the mutilated bodies of German troops killed and left on the road as a warning from partisans.

The partisan movement operated extensively during the Bagration offensive and was actually incorporated into the planning. Since the very early stages of the war on the Eastern Front the Germans had found it very difficult combating partisan activities. In fact just twenty-four hours before the Russian offensive was unleashed the partisans conducted a series of sabotages against important railway networks. In spite of the extensive use of partisan activity leading up to the Russian offensive, a number of German commanders admitted that 'partisan activity was negligible in their area'. However, a number of German accounts admitted that although the partisans operated well in tactical co-operation with regular Red Army units, they were most effective when the German forces were withdrawing or attempting to breakout of the pockets.

One such pocket that drew the attention of the partisans had formed near Pekalin, south of Smolovichi. Three complete divisions composing most of what remained of the XII Corps, which was the 31st, 57th, and 267th and remnants of 25th Panzergrenadier, 78th Assault and 260th divisions, were all trapped. There were also parts of the XXVII Corps ensnared in the pocket along with various stragglers and some 5,000 wounded. Although the bulk of the formations were understrength with no heavy weapons, the 25th Panzergrenadier Division was the strongest with some 52 assault and self-propelled guns. However, both fuel and ammunition was in very short supply, in spite of an airdrop days earlier. In fact ammunition was so low that no more than 10 rounds per gun were issued to the gun crews. With insufficient fuel or ammunition the heavy weapons could not be used effectively, and any hope of breaking out of the pocket appeared futile. However, with the thought of being captured by the Russians, German commanders feverishly began planning a major breakout of the pocket.

Just before midnight on 5 July the 25th Panzergrenadier Division led the breakout of the Pekalin pocket and attempted to smash through the Soviet ring west towards Dzerzhinsk, southwest of Minsk. Fighting was so fierce that the 25th Panzergrenadier Division soon expended all its ammunition and was forced to destroy all its heavy weapons. In spite of the serious lack of ammunition the German units advanced into the incessant Russian gunfire and regardless of the appalling losses they successfully penetrated a Soviet battery. Despite the huge losses the division was the one of the most successful formations to escape and reach the German lines north of Molodechno and south of Vilnius.

During the night of 5 July the 57th Infantry Division with more than 12,000 troops also broke out of the pocket and met fierce enemy resistance. Under heavy unceasing fire units of the division were able to break through and link with remnants of the 'Feldherrnhalle' Division. Both battered divisions crossed the Cherven – Minsk road, where it clashed with more Red Army forces. Over the next couple of days both divisions tried to maintain cohesion, but were forced to fight in small groups until they were finally surrounded and captured.

The other divisions that broke out that night also had a similar fate. The 78th Sturm Division for instance began their escape under a heavy artillery and mortar fire. Hundreds of Russian weapons of all calibre poured a storm of fire onto the advancing division. One German survivor recalled the attack:

> In the surrounding area whole villages disintegrated under a rolling wall of bursting shells. The storm of sound was stupefying. It was like hell on earth, but we had managed to escape through the enemy lines. For our courageous determination we had paid a high price in blood.

Initially the division had succeeded overrunning the Russian positions, but during the morning of 6 July the Red Army units regrouped. Later that day supported by motorised units the Russians prevented any further German success and went onto capture the division along with its commander, General Traut.

One of the last divisions that attempted to escape the pocket was the 267th Infantry Division. Its main objective was to burst out and cross the Orsha-Minsk railway, and then the main road. However, due to fierce Red Army and partisan attacks the survivors of the division were soon rounded up and marched off along the highway to Borisov.

Over the ensuing days a number of German units and stragglers from the pocket tried with varying degrees of courage and determination to reach the German lines. As they endeavoured to break out west the majority of troops were forced to abandon most of their heavy equipment and weapons. As a result there were frequent scenes of chaos and disorganization as they advanced westward along forest roads and paths trying to escape from the jaws of the Red Army.

A MG34 machine gun crew trying to hold its position during heavy fighting with Red Army troops. The MG34 can be seen in its light machine gun mode on a bipod. Even during Bagration German infantry could have considerable staying power against enemy infantry as long as they kept their weapon operational and deployed in good fields of fire.

A StuG III Ausf G approaches a burning house following intensive fighting. Although Army Group Centre was by far numerically the strongest army group in the German Army on the Eastern Front, it also held by far the longest front, 488 miles. Along this front infantry and armour were thinly stretched and assault guns like the StuG III fought continuously trying with varying degrees of success to hold the front and stem the colossal might of the Red Army.

A Tiger I tank has been knocked out of action. Zimmerit anti-magnetic mine paste can be seen coated on the surface of the vehicle's thick armour in order to prevent enemy troops attaching magnetic mines. However, in the case of this Tiger it has probably been knocked out of action by an anti-tank projectile. The main Tigers to see action during Bagration were from the 505th Heavy Tank Battalion.

The crew of a PzKpfw IV Ausf H have expertly camouflaged their vehicle with various pieces of foliage along side a road. The vehicle is more than likely sitting in ambush waiting for an unsuspecting Russian unit to pass by.

Two photographs taken in sequence a few minutes apart showing a StuG III Ausf G halted in a cornfield. The crew have partly covered some of the vehicle with straw in an attempt to help conceal it from enemy observation. With the ever-increasing losses on the battlefield the assault guns and self-propelled guns proved indispensable to the German soldier on the Eastern Front.

A motorcyclist travels through a typical town that has been literally reduced to rubble by Russian bombardment. During their relentless drive in re-conquering territory from the Germans the Red Army had to pay a very high price, not only in blood, but on the villages, towns and cities that they had to raze to the ground in order to neutralise all German resistance.

Through the same decimated town a German troop column moves slowly past destroyed buildings as it tries to escape from the mighty jaws of the Red Army. During Bagration thousands of civilians were made homeless by the German Army's dogged resistance to hold onto as many urbanized areas as possible.

Well-concealed armoured vehicles belonging to an unidentified unit of the 5th Panzer Division near the village of Kostritsa. Here units of the 5th Panzer Division and the 31st Panzergrenadier Regiment fought a series of heavy battles against five rifle divisions of the 11th Guards Army. After a fierce battle lasting a number of hours German infantry were forced to withdraw into the town of Borisov on the night of 29 June.

An artillery tractor during intensive fighting near Borisov. By the end of June the Red Army had had crossed in numerous places north and south of Borisov, and there were no more German reserves capable of counterattacking the bridgeheads. On 30 June Borisov was engulfed in heavy street fighting, and the remaining German forces there that were not slaughtered, retreated by evening.

A StuG III moves along a dusty road. The Ausf G model was last variant to enter service and it undertook sterling service during Bagration. It mounted a very powerful 7.5cm StuK 40 L/48 gun that delivered an enhanced penetration of up to 3.6-inches of 30-degree sloped armour, and 4.3-inches of unsloped armour at 1094-yards. It was also the first variant to be armed with a 7.92mm MG34 machine gun for local defence.

Panzergrenadiers have hitched a lift onboard two SdKfz 251 halftracks. Panzergrenadiers were the German motorized infantry and travelled by motor vehicle rather than on foot. The Panzergrenadiers were considered elite frontline units because of their mobility and the fact that they usually found themselves thrust into battle alongside armoured Panzer divisions. With skill and determination they would advance in trucks and halftracks, which often offered armour protection and mobility.

Two photographs showing the commander of the same self-propelled gun during operations in Byelorussia. The vehicle has been heavily applied with foliage in order to help reduce the risk of enemy aerial observation. By 1944 this method of camouflage was extensively used by all armoured units both on the Eastern and Western Fronts. Whilst travelling by day armoured vehicles were constantly prone to attack and were either compelled to move by night or they heavily camouflage their vehicles for daytime movement.

Infantry together with armoured support withdraw in the face of superior Russian opposition. By the end of June it was soon realised that the Byelorussian operation was more than just a localised attack. Yet OKH were still slow in ordering reinforcements from Army Group North Ukraine. Consequently, the front would have to be defended with existing resources.

Panzergrenadiers onboard halftracks open fire at Russian infantry. The use of motorized infantry was an example of rapid tactical deployment that changed the way battles were fought in Russia. These troops were always on the moved into the thick of battle and provided advancing armour with valuable support

Two PzKpfw IV`s negotiate a typical road in Byelorussia. Although initially when the Russian offensive was launched supplies in the PzKpfw IV were limited, by the end of June a steady trickle of armour had been transported from Army Group North Ukraine in order to try and help bolster the lines and stem the route.

Two soldiers pose for the camera with horses. Throughout the war on the Eastern Front the German Army had been dependent on animal draught. By 1944 that dependency had increased due to the high level of losses in vehicles. From all over German-occupied Europe and the occupied regions of Russia, long columns of vehicles brought in new horses to supplement the dwindling ranks.

A SdKfz 251/10 armed with a 3.7cm Pak36 embroiled in heavy fighting. This particular armoured personnel carrier for a platoon leader provided him with immediate anti-tank support.

The crew of a PzKpfw IV preparing food onboard their vehicle in Byelorussia. Although the PzKpfw IV was upgraded to combat the heavier Russian vehicles, they still found themselves by 1944 continually outclassed by newer Soviet tanks.

A typical German trench system hastily dug by infantry. In this photograph the soldiers are armed with just rifles and supported by a StuG III. Fighting like this was common during Bagration and the determination and courage shown by the soldiers often led to high losses on both sides.

An 8.8cm flak crew during a brief lull in the fighting in Byelorussia. The 8.8cm flak gun proved to be very reliable and versatile weapon during Bagration and was extensively used by flak crews to deal with aerial and ground threats. As a consequence many Russian bombers and fighters were brought down and on the ground the mighty Soviet armoured spearheads were temporarily halted in some places.

A Panther V Ausf A in undergrowth more than likely keeping under cover away from aerial observation. One of the crewmembers can be seen opening the turret rear escape hatch. During Bagration the Panther undertook sterling service in both an offensive and defensive role. Although there were never enough of them to seriously impede the Russian offensive they still managed to cause disruption and knock out many tanks.

An 8.8cm flak gun is about to be fired in anger against Russian positions. The gun was especially designed for a duel purpose role, possessing a very potent anti-tank capability. This anti-tank capability was constantly required as most sectors of the front had barely enough Panzers to oppose the Russian armour, and thus called upon the flak battalions to try and halt the Red Army's relentless advance.

A StuG III advances across a field. This vehicle is armed with the long-barrelled 7.5cm StuK 40 L43 cannon, which delivered an almighty punch. In addition to the main armament the assault gun carries the 7.92mm MG34 machine gun for local defence. Throughout Bagration the StuG proved its worth in the anti-tank defence role and was probably one of the main reasons why the Germans held their positions for so long in some areas.

A Luftwaffe crew onboard an SdKfz 251 halftrack. Although the Luftwaffe field divisions fought relatively well the units that were employed against Soviet troops during Bagration suffered great losses.

One of the many typical defensive positions built along the central sector of the Eastern Front in 1944. By early July many of these well-fortified positions had been evacuated and left to the Russians to occupy.

A well-concealed PzKpfw IV has been camouflaged by using grass and corn from the surrounding field. Whilst out in these vast Russian fields armoured vehicles were prone to constant aerial attack. It was therefore imperative for the crews to use whatever material they had at their disposal in order to help protect their precious armoured vehicles.

A PzKpfw IV can be seen parked beside a house, using the building as additional protection from aerial or ground observation. In total there were some 4,740 Panzers and assault guns assigned to the Eastern Front in June 1944. Of these only 553 were allotted to Army Group Centre, which consisted of only a few PzKpfw IV`s. Later in the offensive further reinforcements from the 4th Panzer Division, which were put on alert and loaded onto trains, increased the number of PzKpfw IVs north of Kovel.

A SdKfz 251/3 Ausf B belonging to Luftwaffe personnel. This crew are more than likely coordinating with aircraft. For Bagration Army Group Centre was provided with Luftflotte 6, and at the start of the offensive this force numbered 452 combat aircraft. Fighter aircraft totalled 40 Me-109`s and bomber strength was 312, of which nearly were all Heinkel He-111s, with a small number of Ju-88`s.

A SdKfz 251 halftrack with Panzergrenadiers onboard pass a burning building during intensive fighting. The performance of the Panzergrenadiers in battle on the Eastern Front was attributed mainly to the halftrack transporting these infantry units onto the battlefield. Despite being lightly armoured, the halftrack could maintain a relatively modest speed and manoeuvre across country and keep up with fast moving armoured spearheads.

During a pause in the long drive into Byelorussia soldiers and drivers relax in the July Russian sun before moving off again. The long column of supply vehicles and two PzKpfw IV`s are a small token gesture of reinforcements destined for the front line in Army Group Centre.

A photograph of a German soldier armed with a MG42 machine gun slung over his right shoulder for ease of carriage. The MG42 was the finest machine gun ever produced and had supreme handling qualities. During the Russian offensive the weapon was used extensively in a defensive role and with its tremendous rate of fire it was quite capable holding an attacking frontage for several miles.

A 3.7cm Flak anti-tank gun, mounted on the back of an artillery tractor is supporting ground forces during heavy fighting. The hinged sides have been completely removed for combat, in order to allow the crew plenty of space to manoeuvre.

German troops can be seen dug-in along a trench during heavy fighting against advancing Soviet forces. By this period of the battle soldiers had to quickly improvise their defensive positions. Normally these defences consisted of nothing more than deep trenches with an assortment of infantry armed with rifles, Panzerfaust anti-tank rockets, or machine guns.

A German soldier poses for the camera during a pause in the fighting. Behind him his vehicle parked next to a building has been heavily camouflaged with branches from a tree.

A commanding officer confers with one of the crewmembers of a SdKfz 251 halftrack. In some sectors of the front communication between the command centres had completely collapsed leaving troop formations often confused and unable to perform their operational duties in cohesive and organised manner.

In a field a group of SdKfz 251 halftracks can be seen along side a halted PzKpfw IV during a lull in the fighting. The SdKfz 251 was used extensively by the Germans during Bagration and it was frequently seen in the thick of battle, moving alongside tanks and providing the latter with valuable support.

A SdKfz 251 is embroiled in fierce fighting as it passes along a road. These vehicles were often moved to the heart of the battlefield where they would debus it troops and go into action before returning to another battle line. As the frontline shifted westward this highly mobile method of troop movement was used widely during the offensive and proved an effective means of moving soldiers from one disintegrating part of the line to another.

A photograph taken earlier in the year of Field Marshal Model, here standing next to a SdKfz 251 halftrack. Model was given command of Army Group Centre on 28 June after General Busch had been sacked by Hitler. Model though still retained control of Army Group North Ukraine, which was under his deputy, General Josef Harpe. By 13 July the Field Marshal had some forty-three divisions, five of them Panzer and one Panzergrenadier, in his two army groups. As the Führer`s `Fireman` Model was determined to stem the Russian onslaught in Army Group Centre, but soon realized that by the time he had taken command, it was already doomed.

Two photographs taken in sequence showing a Luftwaffe vehicle that has a flak gun mounted on the back. Throughout the war, especially during the last years, the Germans constantly improvised and utilized a number of various vehicles to carry anti-tank guns. These flak guns were formidable weapons and able to deal with both low-flying aircraft and ground targets.

Two photographs showing the same commanding officer belonging to one of the Luftwaffe Field Divisions. In both photos he is seen holding a map, and from his staff car he can be seen conferring with one of his officers regarding the next strategic move on the battlefield. The main two Luftwaffe field divisions during Bagration were the 4th and 6th LFD, and these were attached to the Third Panzer Army LIII Corps under the command of General Gollwitzer.

On a road west of the city of Vitebsk a Luftwaffe soldier scours the terrain through a pair of 6 x 30 binoculars. As early as 25 June the 4th Luftwaffe Field Division was severely damaged following its desperate attempt to hold Vitebsk. During the heavy fighting the division attempted to breakout but was smashed to pieces. The remnants of the division fled westward whilst those that were surrounded were captured. Its commanding officer General Pistorius fell in action on 27 June trying to escape the impending slaughter. As for the 6th Luftwaffe Field Division this suffered the same fate. By the end of June both divisions almost ceased to existent with the remaining troops being regrouped into hastily formed *ad hoc* units.

Here the crew of an 8.8cm flak gun can be seen in action against a Russian target. In spite of the terrible losses inflicted upon the German Army during June and July, the troops still proved to be masters of the fighting retreat, giving up ground to the enemy and mounting stinging counterattacks. However, Hitler could never see the benefit of such tactics, usually ordering his units to fight where they stood. Consequently, without the option of flexibility, units suffered horrendous casualties in bludgeoning counterattacks, and by the time Hitler could be persuaded to allow a withdrawal, it was usually too late for an effective counterattack to be launched.

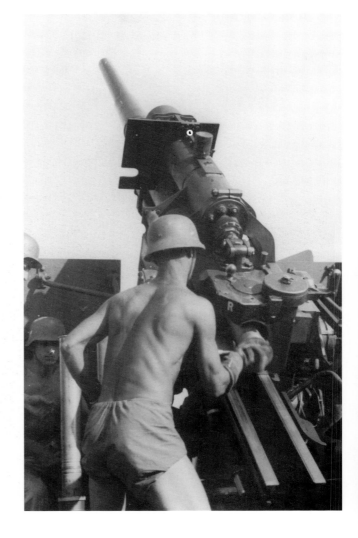

A StuG crewman wearing the familiar special field-grey uniform worn by crews of tank destroyer and self-propelled assault gun units.

Just prior to the moment of firing, an artillery crew are in the process of shelling a Russian position. Although German units fought superbly in battle, there was nothing that they could do to stop the Soviet tide. Even the Panzer divisions were ground down in battles of attrition. Their supply lines were stretched to the limit and beyond, and Germany did not have enough men of military age to make good the battle losses.

The crew of a StuG III rest inside the relative safety a forest with their assault gun. Since early 1943 there had been a massive increase in the production of StuG III`s. Since they were cheaper to build than a Panzer, they were increasingly used as substitutes for Panzers during the last year of the war.

Two halftracks mounting 2cm flak quadruple-barrelled anti-aircraft guns make their way along a dusty road to join a withdrawing column of other armoured vehicles during early July.

A Tiger.I passes through one of the many destroyed towns and villages during Army Group Centres desperate withdrawal towards the borders of Poland and the Baltic state of Lithuania and Latvia. The Tiger tank played a prominent role during the later stages of Bagration, but was hindered by lack of support. As a consequence these monsters were driven from their often meagre positions by overwhelming enemy resistance, and as a consequence a number of them were destroyed in bitter and bloody fighting.

Withdrawal of German troops with a Panther tank from the 4th Panzer Division. (Wydawnictwo Militaria)

Tiger of the 507 Heavy Tank Battalion, Byelorussia, June 1944. (Wydawnictwo Militaria)

Vehicles from the 4th Panzer Division, Byelorussia, June 1944. (Wydawnictwo Militaria)

SU-76M self- propelled gun from the Russian 1223rd SP Artillery Regt, 5th Guards Tank Army in Nowa Wilejka, Poland in July 1944. (Wydawnictwo Militaria)

Russian SU-85 tank destroyer from the 1st Byelorussian Front in the Minsk area, July 1944. (Wydawnictwo Militaria)

German StuG 40 Ausf G, Byelorussia, June 1944. (Wydawnictwo Militaria)

Russian SU-76M SP guns entering Minsk in July 1944. (Wydawnictwo Militaria)

Two Russian SU-76Ms from the 1st Byelorussian Front in June 1944. (Wydawnictwo Militaria)

German StuG 40 Ausf. G on Eastern Front, summer 1944. (Wydawnictwo Militaria)

Waffen SS troops man an anti-tank position with StuG 40 and Pak 38, Russia, June 1944. (Wydawnictwo Militaria)

PART III

Destruction: 6–13 July 1944

Last Battles

In nearly two weeks of continuous fighting Army Group Centre had lost in the region of 25 divisions. Of its original strength of 165,000, Fourth Army reported it had lost a staggering 130,000 men. The Third Panzer Army had lost some 10 divisions. Ninth Army too had lost unprecedented amounts of men and equipment with remnants of its forces trying to escape west towards the German lines. All over Army Group Centre the situation worsened daily as isolated pockets of German troops attempted to breakout and struggle west. Annihilating these pockets became a major objective of the Red Army, and for the next ominous days that followed the last battles of Army Group Centre were played out.

As thousands of German troops tried to escape the slaughter many vicious battles were fought. There were crippling shortages of every kind and the remaining German formations were compelled to break up into smaller detachments and fight to the bitter death. No soldier wanted to fall into the hands of the Russians. They often remarked that they would rather perish on the battlefield, dying a honourable death for Germany, than to be captured and killed. From one collapsed area to another the German soldier fought on outnumbered at least twenty-to-one. Many formations that were encircled were close to annihilation. Stragglers that had managed to escape from the pockets were invariably killed by Russian units combing the area. The Red Army used flame-throwers extensively against stragglers in forests, particularly in clearing out hiding places. They utilised hand grenades more regularly than rifles, and called them their 'pocket artillery'. This had been a highly effective way of reducing pockets of resistance during street fighting, especially at Stalingrad. Now they could blast out areas that were inaccessible or too dangerous to attack on foot.

Virtually along all sectors of the front the Red Army were moving faster than Army Group Centre could deploy its meagre defences. Due to the rapid advance of the Russians even attempting to stand and fight became increasingly difficult. The 1st Baltic Front was now driving towards Dvinsk, the 3rd Byelorussian Front towards Baranovichi and then Molodechno and onto Vilnius and Lida, whilst the 2nd Byelorussian Front stayed behind in the Minsk area to mop up the German pockets and stragglers roaming the countryside.

Both the Second Army and Third Panzer Army in the north were still fighting hard in a number of large-scale battles, and in some areas were actually holding ground because the main Soviet drive had bypassed them. Having achieved the main objective of destroying Army Group Centre the Russians were determined to gain as much ground as possible to the west, thus leaving a number of German formations undefeated, but cut off. Around the Nalibocki forest the Germans held their positions and fought a series of heavy battles to prevent Russian forces from reaching the town of Baranovichi. Over the next couple of days German defensive combat against individual Soviet attacks were relatively successful in spite of the overwhelming firepower. Even the Hungarian forces managed to stem a number of Red Army attacks that were made out of the forest from the south, but the success was only temporary and Russian troops soon forced a withdrawal into the area south of Baranovichi. Elements of the 4th Panzer Division, which were holding positions in the area, were at breaking point. In order to try and stabilise the situation attempts were made to reinforce the garrison in the town, but Russian attacks were so overwhelming that a general evacuation of Baranovichi was immediately ordered on 7 July. Parts of the 4th Panzer Division along with air defence units and the 611th Security Regiment finally left the town. The following day it fell into Russian hands.

With the capture of Baranovichi the focus of effort changed to the north, to the area of Molodechno and Vilnius, which allowed the Red Army more freedom to advance north and westward. The roads west of the town although in not very good condition gave the Russians the chance to attack towards Slonim and Vilnius and widen the deployment of its forces, especially against German blocking units. However, German forces in the area were not going to give up every foot of ground without a fight. On the Baranovichi – Berezovka road heavy fighting broke out as elements of the 4th Panzer Division halted, and tried to contain Red Army units from moving west along the road. The 507th Heavy Tank Battalion counterattacked at Leipciani and what followed was a brutal tank battle between the battalions Tigers and the enemy tanks, in which the Russians suffered very heavy losses. After the successful engagement the battalion withdrew east of the Berezovka forest, which was just west of the town of Derewna.

By 7 July Russian forces were advancing at breakneck speed towards the Lithuanian city of Vilnius. Already the Soviet 5th Guards Tank Army had bypassed the 5th Panzer Division, which was attempting to reach the city. Vilnius was under Hitler's 'Fortified Area' order, and the Führer had already made it perfectly clear to his commanders that it must be held at all costs. Hitler was hoping to defend the city with four Panzer divisions, but was told these could not be assembled before 23 July. It was imperative to hold Vilnius, he said, because without the city it would become a springboard for the Russians to carve its way through Lithuania onto the Baltic Sea shores and then into East Prussia. Without the city he was concerned that it would become almost impossible to re-establish a sustainable connection between the two German army groups.

The fortress of Vilnius was under the command of Luftwaffe General Rainer Stahel, and elements of the Third Panzer Army under the command of General Reinhardt. Over the next few days the German garrison at Vilnius tried to hold out against heavy attacks from the 5th Guards Tank Army. During the night of 10 to 11 July Luftwaffe combat formations with 8.8cm flak guns were committed in the fortress of Vilnius and reported that they had successfully destroyed 30 enemy tanks. However, in spite of a number of successful engagements against the enemy the situation was drastically changing for the worse and it soon became clear that the fortress could no longer hold. Model's drastic attempts to close the gap north and south of the city to help relieve the fortress made no difference whatsoever. Despite the appalling conditions and the chaotic nature of the situation the defenders continued to mercilessly resist enemy attacks for as long as possible. With the position deteriorating by the hour General Stahel, commander of the fortress, proposed to breakout west during the night of 12/13 July.

On 11 July General Stahel received reports that Army Group North was in the process of closing the gap between Army Group Centre with their own forces. Stahel was aware that this army movement would allow the relative safe evacuation of the garrison from the city. During the night of 12/13 July, after destroying all their heavy weapons the fortress broke out of the city in a westerly direction. Almost 3,000 soldiers in total left Vilnius, with many frantically swimming the river to reach lead elements of the 6th Panzer Division. The following day on 13 July, after more than five days of continuous combat, fortress Vilnius was finally captured.

After the fall of Vilnius fighting in the area continued with unabated ferocity. The 6th Panzer Division fought to open a route through to Zysmory, whilst remnants of the IX Army Corps were embroiled in thick fighting near Anyksciai. Losses in the area were terrible.

The destruction of so many troops prompted Model to form 'corps detachments' from battered battalions and organize them into divisions and re-arm them. The Third Panzer Army was given remnants of the 95th Infantry Division, 197th Infantry Division, and the 246th Infantry Division. The Fourth Army were supposed to receive what was left of the 110th Infantry Division, 299th Infantry Division and 267th Infantry Division, whilst the Ninth Army were to receive remnants of the 296th Infantry Division, 134th Infantry Division, and 383rd Infantry Division. The Second Army were to receive the 35th Infantry Division, 129th Infantry Division and the 232nd Infantry Division. As for the other smashed and badly depleted divisions these were moved to defend other parts of the Reich and to relieve the pressure on the Western Front, which was by this stage of the war also causing OKH considerable problems. Below is a list of battered divisions removed from Army Group Centre:

Divisions Removed From Army Group Centre July 1944

6th Infantry Division
12th Infantry Division
31st Infantry Division
45th Infantry Division
78th Assault Division
18th Panzergrenadier Division
25th Panzergrenadier Division
'Feldherrnhalle' Panzergrenadier Division
20th Panzer Division

Model's reinforcements from other worn and badly depleted infantry divisions helped bolster the German formations in spite them being considerably outnumbered in personnel and weapons. The Third Panzer Army, for instance, in the Kovno area, was able to organize a relatively strong defensive position in front of East Prussia with infantry divisions it received. However, despite the determination of Model to organize new defensive lines and strengthen existing formations with remnants of other divisions, he was totally aware that his forces were only capable of containing the enemy for short periods of time. Even during the dying days of Army Group Centre Model constantly tried to reinforce and assemble battle groups to prop up the front. Various battle groups or *Kampfgruppe* were widely used and organized from badly depleted infantry divisions. Generally a battle group was an *ad-hoc* combined arms formation, usually employing combination of tanks, infantry, anti-tank weapons and artillery components. It could range in size from a corps to a company, but most common was a battalion-sized formation. The battle group were generally referred to by either its commanding officer or the parent division. '*Kampfgruppe* Metz' for instance was one of a number of battle groups organized for deployment in Army Group Centre that were primarily formed in order to strengthen the German position and hold the line for as long as possible. This battle group was built from elements of the 170th Infantry Division and with staff from the 221st Security Division.

Formations of 'Kampfgruppe Metz'

170th Infantry Division (elements still arriving)
221st Security Division Staff (included units from *Kampfgruppe* Lendle)
14th Infantry Division *Kampfgruppe*
31st Police Battalion
299th Infantry *Kampfgruppe*
812th Field Commandant
(included elements of the 18th Flak Division)

For the next few days Army Group Centre continued moving slowly west toward Kaunas, the Neman River, and Bialystok. Although there had been urgent appeals from Model for Army Group North to come to his assistance, help did not come. Army Group North could not release the divisions promised for they were already fighting for survival against massive attacks from the 2nd Baltic and 3rd Baltic Front between Dvina and the Velikaya.

By 13 July the Third Panzer and Fourth Armies managed to halt on a line from Ukmerge south of Kaunas and along the Neman to south of Grodno. The Second Army had contested bitterly and was brought back toward Bialystok. The Ninth Army, almost decimated, was licking its wounds along the borders of East Prussia. As for the Red Army, they had covered more than 200 miles without pause, but for the time being had outrun their supplies. This allowed what was left of Army Group Centre to regain some of its strength and reinforce its positions. But the Russians were now deep in territory ravaged by the recent battles against Army Group Centre. With Russia almost liberated, victory was now beckoning for the Red Army.

Two photographs showing a 15cm heavy field howitzer crew during a lull in the fighting. As the standard heavy field howitzer in the German Army, the gun was very effective at demolishing enemy positions. However, in a defensive role the weapon was too heavy and not very effective again rapid enemy movement.

One of the most effective means of moving anti-tank guns quickly from one battle front to another was the use of halftracks, as seen here in this photograph. The most popular Pak guns to see service during Bagration were the Pak 38, Pak 40 and Pak 43. All of these weapons proved hard-hitting, easy to conceal and relatively cheap to produce.

A Luftwaffe 8.8cm flak crew rest during a very warm day in early July 1944. The 8.8cm flak gun was a formidable air-defence weapon. Although less-than-ideal during the Russian offensive owing to its high profile and length of emplacement and displacement time, it still provided the ground forces a general cover against air attack.

A Luftwaffe 8.8cm flak gun in action against an aerial target. In spite of the overwhelming superiority of the Red Army Air Force, German air-defence batteries were able to cause significant damage to fighter and bomber aircraft, especially where there were a number of them emplaced in one area.

The crew of a StuG III converse with another StuG crew during a lull in the battle. By the second week of July armoured crews had been pushed to limit of their endurance. Not only were they exhausted after weeks of constant battle but their vehicles were worn out and fuel and ammunition were becoming increasingly difficult to obtain.

Well concealed in undergrowth a Wespe self-propelled gun is preparing to fire against Red Army positions. This vehicle was one of the most popular self-propelled light howitzers to see action during Bagration. In this photograph one of the crewmembers can be seen looking through his binoculars, deducing the exact location of the enemy to order the gunner to adjust the correct distance and height required to fire the gun.

A 8.8cm flak gun in a defensive position. With the gun elevated to a 90% angle it is more than likely being employed as an *ad-hoc* anti-tank gun. The number of kill rings painted on the barrel clearly indicates its effectiveness against ground targets.

A Nashorn tank destroyer moves through a Russian town. Although the Nashorn undertook sterling defensive fighting during Bagration the Panzer divisions in which it served had been slowly ground down in a number of offensive and defensive actions. This consequently led to most of the assault guns and self-propelled guns being lost.

During Bagration Army Group Centre were provided with a variety of weapons for its tactical air-defence, which included the very effective and deadly 3.7cm quadruple 3.7cm flak gun, seen here in a well defended emplacement.

A well-camouflaged 15cm howitzer is being prepared for firing by its crew. Throughout its early years of service on the battlefield the gun proved a success, but the crews found it far too heavy. By 1944 only a few of these weapons remained in active service and were used mainly in Russia until the end of the war.

Five photographs taken in sequence showing the crew of a 5cm Pak38. The gun itself was of conventional design, fitted with a muzzlebrake and semi automatic breech. The carriage had a split trail with tubular legs and solid-tyre disc wheels. Although initially the Luftwaffe used the Pak 38, it was soon found in the ranks of the German Army. In fact, the gun was destined to become the most widely used anti-tank gun by the Waffen-SS. The Pak 38 was first used in the invasion of the Soviet Union where it was the only gun available which could defeat the T-34 tank. But once again on the Eastern Front anti-tank gunners soon realised that a more powerful gun would be needed to combat the heavier Red Army tanks. Although the Pak 38 was seen in relatively small numbers by 1944, other more powerful Pak guns had long since replaced it like the Pak 40, Pak 41, and the most deadly of them all, the Pak 43.

An 8.8cm Luftwaffe flak crew during operations in mid-July 1944. Of all the flak guns that were introduced into service one of the best-known and reliable weapons was the 8.8cm Flugabwehrkanone 18, 36 und 37 or 8.8cm Flak 18, 36 and 37. It was a very deadly and effective piece of weaponry and scored sizeable hits both in an anti-aircraft role and against ground targets as well. All three versions were extensively used during the war by the Luftwaffe, Wehrmacht and later the Waffen-SS. These three services also used another new 8.8cm Flak gun. It was known as the 8.8cm Flugabwehrkanone 41 or 8.8cm Flak 41 (*Eisenerz*) and was built specifically for a dual-purpose role and thus possessed a genuine anti-tank capability. Its longer 71-calibre barrel gave it an increased muzzle velocity and better penetration. In service it proved robust, reliable, and it continued in production until the end of the war. During Bagration it was extensively used by both the Luftwaffe and German Army.

A Luftwaffe flak crew equipped with a 2cm quadrupled-barrelled self-propelled anti-aircraft gun are in action against a Red Army position. By the time Bagration was unleashed, mechanized formations were well equipped with flak guns. There were motorized flak battalions, with divisions being furnished with additional platoons and companies in the Panzergrenadier, Panzer and artillery regiments. This particular flak gun was a formidable weapon and able to deal with both low-flying aircraft and ground targets.

German vehicles consisting mainly of halftracks are purposely spread out across a field in order to minimise the potential damage caused by an aerial attack. By 1944 it had become common practice for armoured crews to withdraw in this type of formation and thus try and save what vehicles they had left.

An unusual photograph showing a Luftwaffe 8.8cm flak crew posing for the camera, whilst one crewmember is having a shave. Behind the elevated flak gun are `pup` tents, which were a combination of using a number of Zeltbahns to form four man tents as sleeping quarters.

A halftrack is towing a trailer more than likely containing supplies for the front. By the second week of July supplies had dwindled significantly and desperate measures were taken in order to furnish the front with whatever resources they could muster from either the Northern or Southern Army Groups.

Various vehicles and troops withdraw from the receding front under the cover of a PzKpfw IV. The PzKpfw IV was the most common Panzer during Bagration, but was slowly being outclassed by some of the newer Russian tanks.

The crew of a Tiger I has halted, and the crewmembers can be seen scouring the terrain trying to work out the next move of their opponent. The main Tiger tanks to see action during Bagration were attached to the 5th Panzer Division. By German standards the 5th Panzer Division boasted a formidable force, with 70 Panther tanks, 55 Pz Kpfw`s, as well as 29 Tigers of the 505th Heavy Tank Battalion.

An interesting photograph showing the crew of a Tiger I undertaking some extensive maintenance to their vehicle out in the field. Much of the success of the Tiger tanks during the war on the Eastern Front owed much to the independent Tiger battalions that kept the vehicles in fighting condition.

The crew of a PzKpfw IV have attached a steel connecting tow cable to another vehicle after it developed mechanical failure and needed towing to a maintenance workshop. Note the foliage draped on the rear end of the Panzer. This heavy foliage is no doubt due to the continual daily threat posed by the Red Army at this stage of the war.

A StuG III parked inside a village somewhere in Byelorussia in July 1944. By this period of the Russian offensive German armour had been severely mauled. The massive losses resulted from inadequate supplies and not the skill of the defenders.

One of many armoured vehicles destroyed by overwhelming Russian firepower. Here a halftrack has been decimated by an anti-tank gun. In the distance a 15cm howitzer gun carriage can be seen more than likely belonging to another destroyed halftrack.

A Nashorn tank destroyer during defensive operations along the Polish border in July 1944. By this period of the offensive all reserves were gone, the *Panzerwaffe* was now only a shadow of its former self. As logistical problems increased, much of the armour was worn down and in desperate need of being withdrawn and re-equipped. Both Army Group North and Army Group South Ukraine did what they could to help the centre, but they too were experiencing similar problems.

A Luftwaffe 8.8cm flak crew engaged in defending positions against advancing Red Army armour in early July 1944. By this period of the war the 8.8cm flak gun was used extensively in a defensive role against both ground and aerial targets. It was a weapon that was still very much feared by the Russians.

On the outskirts of a bombed out town a Luftwaffe flak crew prepare their hastily prepared positions. One crew member scours the terrain trying to deduce the location of the advancing enemy.

One infantry weapon that was used extensively during Bagration was the single-shot Panzerfaust. These hand held hollow steel firing tubes were very light and mobile and could be fired from a variety of positions; kneeling down and standing with the weapon resting on the firer's shoulder or across his right arm were the most popular.

A StuG III Ausf G with intact side skirts moves along a road passing scattered knocked out Russian tanks. During the last days of Bagration a great number of StuG`s had been lost due to their sterling service supporting the crumbling front lines in a number of determined defensive actions.

A Pak crew in action against advancing Red Army tanks. This was a typical scene in Army Group Centre. Many divisions were now encircled or destroyed. Those that were trapped tried desperately to breakout out, mostly with fatal consequences.

Panzergrenadiers withdraw across a bombed and blasted landscape supported by a StuG III Ausf G. By mid-July Army Group Centre had been smashed to pieces by the Red Army and was now withdrawing into Poland and Lithuania. The Soviets were now determined to bring the offensive over the pre-war Polish border and into Lithuania. The end of Army Group Centre had been cast.

Tiger tank has halted preparing for the coming battle for the Vistula bridgeheads in July 1944. Now that Army Group Centre had been decimated the Red Army was able to make a determined drive into Poland to the River Vistula barrier where it succeeded in securing several small bridgeheads and eventually a major bridgehead at Sandomierz.

A Luftwaffe 8.8cm flak crew in action against a ground target. Throughout Bagration the 8.8cm flak gun often supplemented the divisions lack of Pak guns. Most of these guns, however, were destroyed or were abandoned by the crews having run out of ammunition.

A photograph taken through a range finder showing two Panther tanks moving along a road towards heavy fighting. The Panther was a formidable machine in 1944, and coupled with its great mobility, armour protection and firepower it caused considerable damage to the enemy. However, by the time Bagration was unleashed there were too few Panthers available on the Eastern Front to advert the inevitable destruction of Army Group Centre. [Michael Cremin]

A MG34 machine gun crew are taking cover from enemy fire. Two disabled Russian tanks can be seen. During the offensive the Red Army had hurled more than 2,700 tanks against Army Group Centre, and although there were high losses Soviet armour still had a six-fold advantage over the Germans in armour by the middle of July.

Standing next to a destroyed Russian tank are three German soldiers serving as forward observers. One of the men is using a pair of scissor binoculars, or `donkeys ears`, as they were nicknamed by the troops.

A mortar team delivers fire support against Russian positions. A grenadier battalion's machine gun company possessed a mortar platoon with six mortars along with its three heavy machine gun platoons. This was considered more than enough firepower to stem the enemy for a period of time.

On a congested road are a number of Panther V Ausf A`s belonging to the 4th Panzer Division. Although small in numbers the Panther fought extremely well and scored sizeable kills against Russian armour. Combat survivability of the Panther owed much to its thick armoured plating, lethal 7.5cm gun, and its Panther tactics known as *Panzerglocke*. This was a bell-shaped attacking formation with armoured engineers following up the lead Panthers and Tigers.

Here is a captured Russian Katyusha rocket launcher mounted on the back of a tracked vehicle. These 16-rail rocket launchers were not a precision weapon, but could dump 300 kg of explosive on the target with lethal consequences. Katyusha rockets were used abundantly during Bagration and were able to inflict heavy losses.

At dawn a company of 3.7cm quadruple flak guns can be seen during defensive operations in Poland East of the Vistula River. A typical German infantry division in 1944 consisted of a motorised flak company equipped with at least 12 x 2cm or 3.7cm flak guns.

A young flak crew in one of the many defensive positions that covered Army Group Centres receding front lines. Due to the severe lack of armour much of the fighting was heavily supported by flak crews or MG34 and MG42 machine gun nests.

During the defence of Poland in August 1944 troops from the Hermann Goring Division are seen. The elite Herman Goring Division was rushed to Poland after the destruction of Army Group Centre in a desperate attempt to stem the Russian onslaught across the Vistula River south of Warsaw. In spite of dogged determination from the Division Red Army forces managed to establish a firm bridgehead near Magnuszew.

Here StuG crews have halted during a lull in fighting in early July 1944. Although the StuG.III was regarded as an effective weapon against the mighty Red Army, the open terrain coupled with inadequate support caused unprecedented amounts of losses in Army Group Centre.

Aftermath

The fate of Army Group Centre, July 1944

With nothing but a string of defeats and unable to avert the terrible situation Model finally informed OKH that Army Group Centre could no longer assemble a projected attack north of Vilnius in time to halt the Russian armour – Army Group North would have to do it and suffer the consequences.

By the third week of July 'Operation Bagration' had fulfilled its objectives and had left Army Group Centre almost totally destroyed. The rapid Russian advance had taken the Army Group by complete surprise and had consequently bypassed a number of large German troop concentrations on the frontline in the Third Panzer Army and the Ninth Army sectors. Although remnants of these forces managed to claw their way west to the relative safety of Army Group North, its once proud forces were a mere shadow of their former selves. The badly beaten and bruised divisions had arrived east of Lithuania and to the east of the frontier of Poland with most of its units crushed. Between 25 and 30 divisions were mauled in three weeks of continuous combat with 17 of the divisions totally annihilated. Losses in troops were estimated in the region of over 300,000. Of those 150,000 were captured, of which more than half were killed on their way to POW camps, or later died of disease or starvation. On 17 July the Russians paraded some 57,000 German prisoners through the main streets of Moscow to celebrate their victory in Byelorussia. The conquest of Byelorussia had caused a huge sacrifice in men. The First Byelorussian Front had suffered the most with the loss of some 66,000 soldiers. On all fronts the total causalities amounted in excess of 178,000 Russian troops.

The annihilation of Army Group Centre was without doubt the greatest defeat of the German Army during World War Two. Its terrible collapse was so devastating that is was far worse than the defeat at Stalingrad eighteen months earlier. Even along the shores of Normandy when the Western Allies undertook their greatest amphibious landing of all time, the attack was regarded as a mere shadow, compared to what was about to be unleashed 1300 miles away on the Eastern Front three weeks later.

The destruction of Army Group Centre was certainly the main contributor to the demise of the Wehrmacht in the East. It had created a massive vacuum due to the terrible losses of men and equipment. To plug the huge open gaps OKH were forced to move divisions from both Army Group North and Army Group North Ukraine. The movement of these forces were undertaken with the utmost speed as reports confirmed that the Russians were preparing to launch their third phase of the summer strategic offensive. It was known as the Lublin-Brest operation and its objective was to hurl the First Byelorussian Front towards Lublin and the River Vistula in Poland. The offensive was unleashed on 18 July and the most successful of these attacks was made by Konev's 1st Ukrainian Front. It was the single most powerful front in the Red Army with over one million soldiers including 1,614 tanks and assault guns, 14,000 guns and mortars and over 2,000 aircraft.

In front of both the 1st Byelorrussian and 1st Ukrainian Fronts was Army Group North Ukraine, which consisted of 34 infantry divisions, five Panzer divisions and one motorised division. During the early part of the summer the Army Group had been comparable in strength to that of the 1st Ukrainian Front, but the aftermath of 'Bagration' had left the army understrength due to a number of units being pulled in to try help stem the Russian advance through Byelorussia.

On 13 July the Red Army unleashed its mighty force against Army Group North Ukraine, and over the coming days the Russians systematically ground down the German units using heavy ground and aerial bombardments. By 18 July Soviet armoured spearheads mashed their way through from the north and south and met on the River Bug just thirty miles west of Lwow. Behind them the XIII Corps consisting of five German divisions and the Waffen-SS Division Galicia, were encircled. As panic and confusion swept the front lines German troops begun moving toward the River Bug, finalising their withdrawal into Poland.

During the second half of July whilst Army Group North Ukraine tried its best to hold positions on the River Bug, remnants of Army Group Centre were attempting to create a solid front on the line Kaunas, Bialystok-Brest and assemble its forces on both its flanks. They intended to strike north and south to restore contact with both neighbouring army groups. Remnants of Army Group Centre were too weak to avoid the deteriorating situation and by the last week of July the Russians rolled west through its shattered front, bearing down toward the River Vistula. During this period the Red Army managed a steady advance and soon enabled its forces to be within striking distance of the Vistula River. By the end of the month the Soviet forces were approaching the east bank of the Vistula and had successfully secured a bridgehead in the suburbs of Warsaw.

From a military standpoint by the end of July 1944 Army Group Centre ceased to exist. Its destruction was now to have a profound effect on the entire operation on the Eastern Front. Army Group North Ukraine was now fighting for survival, whilst Army Group North was attempting to defend the Baltic from capture.

But in spite of the terrible situation left by the destruction to the centre of the front, by incredible efforts of military skill and courage, coupled with the fact that the Red Army's offensive had slowed down, the frontline on the central sector of the Eastern Front was temporarily stabilized. In no more than six weeks the Russians had bulldozed its way westward covering more than 450-miles, and in the process smashed to pieces Army Group Centre finally halting east of Warsaw, having outrun its supplies.

With the disintegration of Army Group Centre a staunch German defence was now required in order to contain the Red Army and thus prevent it from continuing its tumultuous advance and reaching the borders of the homeland. Over the coming months furious battles raged along the entire German front with remnants of Army Group Centre bearing the brunt of the attacks.

By the end of October 1944 Army Group Centre, still battered and bruised from months of ceaseless combat was desperately trying to hold its positions. What was left of General Rauss's Third Panzer Army and General Hossbach's Fourth Army held a salient in the north while further south along the River Narew was General Weiss's Second Army. Along the front from Modlin to Kaschau were troops of Army Group A, with Ninth Army trying its best to hold onto either side of Warsaw. At Baranov Fourth Panzer Army was facing very strong Russian forces. The Seventeenth Army was positioned between the Vistula and the Beskide, whilst General Heinrici's First Panzer Army was tried to contain its positions in the area of Kaschau and Jaslo.

The German forces that were left fighting on the Eastern Front were now carrying the deep scars left by the destruction of Army Group Centre. With great fortitude and the will to survive its remnants continued fighting the vast tide of the Red Army right to the gates of Berlin six months later.

APPENDIX I

German Organisation 1944

Infantry Division 1944

By 1944 the infantry division had gone through a series of changes and had been modified and reorganised. The reconnaissance battalion, for instance, was removed and replaced with a bicycle-mounted reconnaissance platoon within every regiment. The anti-tank battalion was more or less made motorised and consisted of an anti-tank company equipped with Jagdpanzer IVs, Hetzers or StuGs, which were organised into three platoons of 4 vehicles and a HQ section of 2 vehicles, a motorised anti-tank company of 12 x 7.5cm Pak 40 guns and a motorised flak company equipped with 12 x 2cm or 3.7cm flak guns. The engineer battalion also took over the responsibility of the heavy weapons company. It comprising three engineer companies, each equipped with 2 x 8.1cm mortars, 2 x MGs and 6 portable flamethrowers. The heavy weapons in the engineer battalion were normally mounted in trucks, but by 1944 they were predominately pulled by animal draught, whilst the troops would be mounted on bicycles.

At regimental level an anti-tank company was added. This consisted of a platoon equipped with 3 x 5cm Pak 38 guns and 2 platoons armed with Panzerfausts. Within the regiments, the infantry battalion were reduced in size to just two. A number of divisions in the field were assigned fusilier battalions, structured identically to the new standard rifle battalion. The infantry battalions were equipped with 4 x 12cm heavy mortars, whilst the rifle companies' heavy weapons platoons were equipped with 2 x 8.1cm mortars.

Panzergrenadier Division 1944

By 1944 many infantry divisions were re-designated as Panzergrenadier divisions. Although having an armoured designation, the Panzergrenadier division was still technically an infantry formation. However, unlike a normal infantry division there was a higher than usual attachment of armoured vehicles. A typical Panzergrenadier division had at least one battalion of infantry that were transported to the forward edge of the battlefield by SdKfz.251 halftracks, and various armoured support provided by its own StuG Battalion. A typical Panzergrenadier division normally comprised a HQ company, a motorised engineer battalion and two Panzergrenadier regiments. Invariably a Panzergrenadier division had a StuG Battalion, which contained a HQ Platoon equipped with 3 StuGs, and 3 StuG Companies. The StuG battalion was normally supported by a company comprising a StuG platoon which was equipped with 4 x StuGs with 10.5cm guns, a flak platoon with 3 x quad 2cm guns mounted on SdKfz.6 or 7 halftracks, an armoured engineer platoon with 5 x SdKfz.250 halftracks, and a motorised signal platoon. Other support elements with the divisions comprised the following:

Artillery Regiment

3 x 2cm Flak guns towed by a howitzer battalion
3 x 2cm Flak guns
4 x 15cm sFH 18 Howitzers
4 x 10.5cm leFH 18 Howitzers
1 battery of 6 x Hummels
2 batteries of 6 x Wespe
1 company of 14 x Jagdpanzers
15 x 7.5cm Pak 40 vehicle towed guns
1 company of 12 x Quad Flak 2cm guns
2 companies of 4 x 8.8cm guns

Armoured Reconnaissance Battalion

4 Platoons of 4 x SdKfz.231
MG Platoons of 4 x MG 34/42 [on sustained fire mounts]
3 x Rifle Platoons

Armoured Reconnaissance Battalion Support

2 x 7.5cm le IG 18 guns
3 x 5cm Pak 38 guns
1 x Engineer Platoon

Panzer/Panzergrenadier Brigade July 1944

By early July 1944, as the situation in Army Group Centre deteriorated, Hitler decided that his forces needed small, mobile, fast armoured *Kampfgruppen*, which could be used effectively in action to meet the attacking enemy armoured formations. During the first week of July plans were issued to create these special armoured *Kampfgruppen*. They were to consist of at least one SPW (or armoured half-track) battalion; one Panzer group with some 40 Panzers, one Pak Company and a number of flak guns. In total about twelve such *Kampfgruppen*, named Panzer Brigades, were to see service on the Eastern Front.

On 11 July OKH issued orders to create ten Panzer Brigades and these were designated as Panzer Brigade 101 to 110. Each Panzer Brigade had one Panzer Abteilung with three Panther companies and one Panzer Jaeger Company, and one Panzergrenadier Battalion with four companies.

Panzer/Panzergrenadier Battalion 1944

Battalion Headquarters – 4 officers and 21 men
Communications Platoon – 1 officer and 22 men

Supply Company – 7 officers and 142 men
Supply Detachment (1 officer, 31 men)
Company HQ – 2 officers and 11 men
Maintenance Detachment – 3 officers and 71 men
Fuel Detachment – 11 men
Medical Detachment – 1 officer and 4 men
Munitions Detachment – 14 men

Heavy Company – 4 officers and 143 men
Company HQ – 1 officer and 18 men
Heavy Gun Platoon – 1 officer and 31 men
Two 12 cm Mortar Platoons, each comprising: 1 officer and 47 men
Two Rifle Companies – 3 officers and 187 men, each comprising:
    Company HQ – 1 officer and 20 men
    Heavy Platoon comprising:
        Platoon HQ – 1 officer and 6 men
        Mortar Group – 15 men
        Gun Group – 8 men
        Heavy Machine Gun Group – 13 men
        Flak Group – 12 men
    Three Rifle Platoons, each comprising:
        Platoon HQ – 1 officer or NCO and 7 men
        Three Rifle Squads, each comprising: 10 men
Total Strength of 724 all ranks – 22 officers and 702 men

Heavy Company – 4 officers and 143 men
Company HQ – 1 officer and 18 men
Heavy Gun Platoon – 1 officer and 31 men
Two 12 cm Mortar Platoons, each comprising: 1 officer and 47 men

Flak Company – 3 officers and 96 men
Company HQ – 1 officer and 17 men
Three Flak Platoons, each comprising: 1 officer or NCO and 26 men

Rifle Company – 3 officers and 143 men
Company HQ – 1 officer and 17 men
Two Flak Platoons, each comprising: 1 officer or NCO and 26 men
Two Rifle Platoons, each comprising:
    Platoon HQ – 1 officer or NCO and 6 men
    Three Rifle Squads, each comprising 10 men

Two Rifle Companies, each comprising 4 officers and 145 men
Company HQ – 1 officer and 17 men
Heavy Platoon comprising:
    Platoon HQ – 1 officer and 6 men
    Mortar Group – 15 men
    Gun Group – 8 men
    Flak Platoon – 1 officer and 26 men
Two Rifle Platoons, each comprising:
    Platoon HQ – 1 officer or NCO and 6 men
    Three Rifle Squads, each comprising 10 men
Total Strength of 932 all ranks – 30 officers and 902 men

Typical Panzer Division 1944

15,943 men
91 × Panzer IV (7.5cm L/48 guns) medium tanks
90 × Panther (7.5cm L/70 guns) medium tanks
42 × Hetzer (7.5cm L/48 guns) tank destroyers
9 × 15cm FH 18/40 towed howitzers
18 × 10.5cm leF 18 towed howitzers
6 × 15cm self-propelled sIG infantry guns
12 × 7.5cm Pak 40 towed antitank guns
36 × 5cm Pak39 towed antitank guns
14 × 8.8cm Flak 36 towed antiaircraft guns
12 × 3.7cm Flak 36 towed antiaircraft guns
13 × 2cm towed antiaircraft guns
32 × 7.5cm le. IG 37 and sIG 33 towed infantry guns
80 x 8.1cm mortars
570 x machine-guns
48 x SdKfz 232 and 263 armoured cars
1000 x trucks

Panzer Division
HQ
Reconnaissance Battalion
Self-Propelled Anti-Tank Battalion
Combat Engineer Battalion
Anti-Aircraft Artillery Battalion
Tank Regiment (2 Tank Battalions)
Mechanized Infantry Regiment (Mechanized Infantry Battalion (half-tracks), Road Motorized Infantry Battalion (trucks))
Mechanized Infantry Regiment (Road Motorized Infantry Battalion (trucks), Infantry Battalion)
Artillery Regiment (3 Artillery Battalions)

Panzers, Assault guns and tank destroyers

The following is a list of all the main German armoured fighting vehicles that saw action during Bagration.

PzKpfw IV

The PzKpfw IV was the most popular Panzer used on the Eastern Front and remained in production throughout the war. Despite the huge numbers of enemy tanks arrayed against it the PzKpfw IV continued to demonstrate its superiority on the battlefield and performed well, temporarily halting the Soviet advance. Three variants of the PzKpfw IV that saw extensive service during mid 1944 were the Ausf.G, Ausf.H and Ausf.J. They were all armed with the powerful 7.5cm L/48 gun, and built with improved all-round armoured plating.

PzKpfw V Panther

The Panther tank was a potent fighting weapon and was far the best German tank on the Eastern Front in 1944. Despite initial mechanical problems a year earlier at Kursk the vehicle soon earned its reputation as a deadly adversary to the T–34/85 tank. The success of the new improved Panther Ausf D variant saw the development of the Ausf A. By 1944 the Panther dominated the battlefield and by the time the Russians began their summer offensive great demands were put on it to fill the frontlines. The final Panther variant that entered service was the Ausf G, which was further modified with sloped instead of vertical armour on the lower hull sides. It was also given additional armoured protection that was thickened to 5cm. All three variants were armed with a powerful long-barrelled 7.5cm KwK L/70 gun.

PzKpfw VI Tiger I

Probably the most famous Panzer that saw action on the Eastern Front was the Tiger I. The Tiger was built primarily in response to the heavy and powerful Soviet tanks such as the KV 1 and T–34. This massive machine mounted a lethal long-barrelled 8.8cm KwK 43 L/56 gun. During Bagration it played prominent roles in a number of major defensive battles that were fought against numerically superior Soviet forces. However, the new heavy Russian tanks begun to outclass the Tiger I and heavy losses markedly reduced its effectiveness in Army Group Centre.

StuG III Assault Gun

The most popular armoured fighting vehicle in Army Group Centre in 1944 was the StuG III assault gun. The most common variant to see action during this period was the StuG III Ausf G. This version was armed with the long-barrelled 7.5cm StuK L/48 gun and armed with an MG34 machine gun for local defence. By this period of the war the StuG III, however, was continually hard-pressed on the battlefield and constantly called upon for offensive and defensive fire support, where it was gradually compelled to operate increasingly in an anti-tank role. By the time it saw action during Bagration the StuG III was already being slowly absorbed into the Panzer units, Panzer and Panzergrenadier divisions of the German Army. However, in spite of the assault gun's numerous advantages, equipping some of the Panzer units did not blend well with the nature of the *Panzerwaffe*. Yet, because of the lack of tanks in the dwindling ranks of the Panzer divisions in Army Group Centre, the StuG III was used alongside the Panzer until the end of the war.

Wespe Self-Propelled Gun

The Wespe was armed with a 10.5cm light field howitzer in an open box-like structure attached to a chassis of an old PzKpfw II. The Wespe was a successful self-propelled gun and during Bagration it played a significant role in a number of major offensive and defensive actions. It was the most common German self-propelled light howitzer employed on the Eastern Front during the summer of 1944. Although it had a good off-road capability, it still required a certain amount of skill to manoeuvre as the gun was nose-heavy, which made steering difficult at times.

Nashorn Self-Propelled Gun

The Nashorn was another self-propelled gun that was almost as popular as the Wespe during Bagration. This tank destroyer was built on the chassis of a PzKpfw III/IV and was armed with an 8.8cm Pak 43 duel anti-tank/anti-aircraft gun, and was probably one of the best all round weapons seen on the battlefield during the Russian summer offensive of 1944.

Hummel Self-Propelled Gun

The Hummel self-propelled gun mounted a standard 15cm heavy field howitzer in a lightly armoured rear-fighting compartment built on top of a PzKpfw III/IV tank chassis. It was constructed exactly the same as the Nashorn except it was armed with a different gun. In Army Group Centre the Hummel was used, as was the Nashorn, by the Panzer divisions. There was a battery of six in each division.

Parachute Division 1944

Divisional Headquarters
Three Parachute Regiments, each comprising:
Regimental HQ
Three Parachute Battalions
Heavy Mortar Company – 9 x 12 cm mortars in three Platoons
Anti Tank Company – with a third 8.8 cm Platoon.

Artillery Regiment
Two Light Battalions – 12 x 10.5 cm guns each
One Medium Battalion – 12 x 15 cm guns
Heavy Mortar Battalion – 36 x 12 cm weapons in three Companies each of three Platoons of four

Combat Support
Pioneer Battalion (mainly motorised)
Anti Tank Battalion
Anti Aircraft Battalion – 18 x 2 cm and 12 x 8.8 cm guns in batteries of six
Reconnaissance Company

Flak guns

German anti-aircraft artillery or flak guns were primarily used during the war to defend a position against attacking aircraft. The production of the flak guns contained less variety of weaponry than some of the other classes of artillery that were used, especially during the latter part of the war. By June 1944 there were some 45,550 guns, 30,463 of which were light weapons. However, by this period of the war flak gun crews were already using a variety of weapons to combat not only aerial attacks but ground targets as well. The anti-aircraft guns were primarily designed to deliver a barrage of exploding shells against enemy aircraft. The effectiveness of such flak fire generally required firing literally thousands of rounds of ammunition in order to prevent the enemy aircraft from completing their mission successfully. The success of the flak gun on the Eastern Front saw a large increase in the number of flak units. During 1943 Panzergrenadier regiments received regimental light flak companies. These included self-propelled 3.7cm medium flak guns and quadruple 2cm guns.

By late 1943 and early 1944, both the Wehrmacht and Waffen-SS mechanised formations had become very well equipped with flak guns. Apart from a five-battery motorised flak battalion, divisions also had additional flak platoons and companies in their Panzergrenadier, Panzer and artillery regiments. A typical Panzer division in 1944 for instance was authorised with some 80 towed and 40 self-propelled 2cm guns, six 2cm quadruple weapons, nine 3.7cm guns and 12 heavy 8.8cm flak weapons.

Pak guns

One of the most important defensive and offensive tactics for the Wehrmacht during the war was its ability to counter enemy armour on the battlefield. For this reason the Germans used a variety of mobile weapons capable of firing a solid shot at high velocity so that it could delay the penetrate the armour of enemy tanks. One of the most popular weapons still in service by 1944 was the 5cm Pak 38. The gun itself was of conventional design, fitted with a muzzlebrake and semi automatic breech. The carriage had a split trail with tubular legs and solid-tyre disc wheels. It was so popular that it was found in the Luftwaffe field divisions and in the ranks of the Wehrmacht and Waffen-SS.

Another weapon to see extensive service with the Wehrmacht and Waffen-SS troops in Russia was the 7.5cm *Panzerabwehrkanone* 40 or 7.5cm Pak 40 (*Hünengrab*). The gun was virtually an enlarged version of the Pak 38, using the similar split-trail and a double skinned splinter shield. It became the standard anti-tank gun of the war and because it was relatively cheap to produce it remained in production until 1945. Even in Army Group Centre they proved their worth especially in the hands of well-trained anti-tank gunners.

Whilst the Pak 40 undertook sterling service, there were other more powerful anti-tank guns that were used to confront the ever increasing heavy Soviet tanks, such as the Krupp designed 8.8cm *Panzerabwehrkanone* 43 or 8.8cm Pak 43 (*Neuntoter*). This became the finest anti-tank gun to enter service in the ranks of the Wehrmacht and Waffen-SS. When it arrived at the front for the first time in 1944, it was capable of knocking out any tank in service during this period of the war. The gun was so efficient and deadly it even proved superior to that of the improvised dual-purpose 8.8cm Flak 41. The powerful long 71-calibre barrel with muzzlebrake could be fired from its firing platform while limbered, though over restricted traverse. But in spite of its very useful tactical capability in which it scored sizeable hits against the enemy, the Pak 43 was not cheap, and as a consequence was in short supply.

Despite the ever-increasing production and utilisation of the duel purpose flak guns and captured weapons, there were never enough anti-tank guns to protect the German divisions that were exposed almost daily to the full rigours of enemy warfare. Nonetheless, the Germans continued to fight on with what they had at their disposal, displaying much skill and élan in the process.

APPENDIX II

Hitler's Operation Order No.8

Issued by Army Group Centre
Distribution: 3, 5 copies
This message passes on to Army Commander
The Führer orders to Army Group Centre

To ensure security, their tactical content is to be passed to corps and divisional commanders orally and only to the extent that it concerns them. The Führer's other requirements are to be passed on in an appropriate manner to all ranks. The orders are to be destroyed once read and understood. The orders for the fortified positions of Bobruisk and Mogilev under Fuhrer Order No.11 are not affected by these orders.

(Signed) BUSCH
HQ ARMY GROUP CENTRE

Operation Order No.8

Instructions for the further conduct of operations by Army Group Centre.

The enemy advance on Army Group Centre's sector must now be halted once and for all. To this end I have ordered reinforcement with panzer and infantry divisions, assault gun brigades from other Army Groups and from Germany, this on a scale and at a pace only to be achieved at the cost of weakening other fronts. I have also reinforced 6th Air Force to an extent which makes it by far the stronger air force on the Eastern Front. What I now expect of the Army Group is; however, that no yard of ground shall be given up without fighting for it, and that every commander and man in the Army Group shall have instilled in him the iron will to hold firm. The furthermost line at which the Russian offensive must be halted, cost what it may, is as follows: Lake Chervonoye – Lyuban – Star Dorogi – Osipovichi – River Svisloch – River Beresina to Beresina – Lake Lukomlskoye – present position of 3rd Panzer Army. To the extent that the enemy has already passed this line, he is to be thrown back forthwith by the ruthless employment of all available troops. To the extent that this line may be forced back further, it is to be restored gradually by whatever means possible in short, rigidly controlled bounds. Our troops must make it a point of honour to take all their equipment with them. Ground ceded to the enemy is to be scorched as far as possible; any weapons and stores that our troops are forced to leave behind must be completely destroyed. The task of the Panzer formations, following the principles whose success is so well proven, is to destroy enemy groups that have forced their way forward by a series of swift, sharp punches. I forbid the use of panzer formations in containing positions.

My detailed orders are as follows:

1. Three counterstroke groups are to be formed:
    a. In 9th Army area, 12th and 20th Pz.Div under HQXXXXI Pz. Corps
    b. In the 4th Army area, 5th Pz. Div and 505th Heavy Tank Btn (Tiger), under command of Lt-Gen von Saucken; to this end HQXXXIX Pz. Corps is to be placed at his disposal for the time being.
    c.. In the 3rd Panzer Army's area, 212th Inf. Div and 227th and 232nd Assault Gun Brigades.
    d. A decision on the employment of 4th Pz. Div will be taken at the appropriate time.

2. 9th Army is to restore a continuous front on its sector by pulling back centre and left and making offensive use of its mobile formations. During these operations, it must not lose contact with 4th Army's right. The critical factor here is 4th Army's rate of movement.

3. 4th Army is to fall back by short bounds with a continuous front on to the line River Beresina – Lake Lukomlskoye. In doing this, it must use mobile formations to support its flank. Mogilev and Orsha are to be held for

at least a matter of days, so as to tie down enemy forces and thus facilitate the build-up of the final defensive front further to the rear. Every man in these garrisons must be made aware of the decisive importance of this task.

4. 3rd Panzer Army is to continue holding its present positions or, as needs be, to fight itself clear. Under no circumstances must it let itself be forced further back.

I am confident that the Army Group will do everything in its power to accomplish the task set it. I expect my confidence to be justified.

Signed ADOLF HITLER
Authenticated, Lieut

Army Group Centre Order of Battle 15 June 1944

Army Group Centre
Reserves
707th Infantry Division
14th Infantry Division

OKH Reserves
Panzer Group 'F'
221st Security Division
391st Security Division

SECOND ARMY
Reserves
5th Hungarian Reserve Division
23rd Hungarian Reserve Division
4th Cavalry Brigade
1st Hungarian Cavalry Division

VIII Army Corps
5th Jäger Division
211th Infantry Division
12th Hungarian Reserve Division

XX Army Corps
3rd Cavalry Brigade

XXIII Army Corps
7th Infantry Division
203rd Security Division

NINTH ARMY
LV Army Corps
102nd Infantry Division
292nd Infantry Division

XXXXI Panzer Corps
129th Infantry Division
35th Infantry Division
36th Infantry Division

XXXV Army Corps
45th Infantry Division
383rd Infantry Division
6th Infantry Division

296th Infantry Division
134th Infantry Division
129th Infantry Division

FOURTH ARMY
Reserves
286th Security Division

XII Army Corps
57th Infantry Division
267th Infantry Division
18th Panzergrenadier Division

XXXIX Panzer Corps
31st Infantry Division
12th Infantry Division
337th Infantry Division
110th Infantry Division

XXVII Army Corps
260th Infantry Division
25th Panzergrenadier Division
78th Sturm Division

THIRD PANZER ARMY
Reserves
201st Security Division
95th Infantry Division

VI Army Corps
256th Infantry Division
299th Infantry Division
197th Infantry Division

LIII Army Corps
206th Infantry Division
6th Luftwaffe Field Division
4th Luftwaffe Field Division
246th Infantry Division

IX Army Corps
Division Group '252

APPENDIX IV

Army Group Centre Order of Battle 23 June 1944

Commanders

General Field Marshal E. Busch
General Field Marshal W.Model (from 28 June 1944)

Army Group Centre Reserves

707th Security Division
14th Infantry Division
20th Panzer Division
Panzer Grenadier Division 'Feldherrnhalle'

SECOND ARMY

Reserves

5th Hungarian Reserve Division
23rd Hungarian Reserve Division
4th Cavalry Brigade
1st Hungarian Cavalry Division

VIII Army Corps

5th Jäger Division
211th Infantry Division
12th Hungarian Reserve Division

XX Army Corps

3rd Cavalry Brigade

XXIII Army Corps

7th Infantry Division
203rd Security Division

NINTH ARMY

LV Army Corps

102nd Infantry Division
292nd Infantry Division

XXXXI Panzer Corps

35th Infantry Division
36th Infantry Division
12th Infantry Division

XXXV Army Corps

6th Infantry Division
45th Infantry Division

134th Infantry Division
129th Infantry Division
296th Infantry Division
383rd Infantry Division

FOURTH ARMY

Reserves

286th Security Division

XII Army Corps

18th Panzergrenadier Division
57th Infantry Division
267th Infantry Division

XXXIX Panzer Corps

12th Infantry Division
31st Infantry Division
110th Infantry Division
337th Infantry Division

XXVII Army Corps

25th Panzergrenadier Division
78th Sturm Division
260th Infantry Division

THIRD PANZER ARMY

Reserves

201st Security Division
95th Infantry Division

VI Army Corps

197th Infantry Division
256th Infantry Division
299th Infantry Division

LIII Army Corps

4th Luftwaffe Field Division
6th Luftwaffe Field Division
206th Infantry Division
246th Infantry Division

IX Army Corps

Division Group '252'

Red Army Order of Battle 23 June 1944

1st Baltic Front

4th Assault Army

83rd Rifle Corps
16th Rifle Division
119th Rifle Division
332nd Rifle Division
360th Rifle Division

6th Guards Army

2nd Guards Rifle Corps
9th Guards Rifle Division
166th Rifle Division

22nd Guards Rifle Corps
90th Guards Rifle Division
47th Guards Rifle Division
51st Guards Rifle Division

23rd Guards Rifle Corps
51st Guards Rifle Division
67th Guards Rifle Division
71st Guards Rifle Division

103rd Rifle Corps
29th Rifle Division
270th Rifle Division

Army Artillery
8th Guards Artillery Division
21st Breakthrough Artillery Division

43rd Army

1st Rifle Corps
179th Rifle Division
306th Rifle Division

60th Rifle Corps
357th Rifle Division
235th Rifle Division
334th Rifle Division

92nd Rifle Corps
145th Rifle Division
204th Rifle Division

1st Tank Corps
89th Tank Brigade
117th Tank Brigade
159th Tank Brigade

3rd Air Army

11th Fighter Aviation Corps
5th Guards Fighter Aviation Division
190th Fighter Aviation Division [includes independent air units]

3rd Byelorussian Front

5th Artillery Corps
2nd Guards Breakthrough Division
20th Guards Breakthrough Division
4th Guards Gun Artillery Division

11th Guards Army

8th Guards Rifle Corps
5th Guards Rifle Division
26th Guards Rifle Division
83rd Guards Rifle Division

16th Guards Rifle Corps
1st Guards Rifle Division
11th Guards Rifle Division
31st Guards Rifle Division

36th Guards Rifle Corps
16th Guards Rifle Division
18th Guards Rifle Division
84th Guards Rifle Division

2nd Tank Corps
25th Guards Tank Brigade
26th Guards Tank Brigade
4th Guards Tank Brigade

Army Artillery
7th Guards Mortar (Multiple Rocket) Division

5th Army

45th Rifle Corps
159th Rifle Division
184th Rifle Division
338th Rifle Division

65th Rifle Corps
97th Rifle Division

144th Rifle Division
371st Rifle Division

72nd Rifle Corps
63rd Rifle Division
215th Rifle Division
277th Rifle Division
2nd Tank Brigade
153rd Tank Brigade

Army Artillery
3rd Guards Breakthrough Artillery Division

31st Army

36th Rifle Corps
173rd Rifle Division
220th Rifle Division
352nd Rifle Division

39th Army

5th Guards Rifle Corps
17th Guards Rifle Division
19th Guards Rifle Division
91st Guards Rifle Division
251st Guards Rifle Division

84th Rifle Corps
158th Rifle Division
164th Rifle Division
262nd Rifle Division
28th Tank Brigade

5th Tank Army

3rd Guards Tank Corps
3rd Guards Tank Brigade
18th Guards Tank Brigade
19th Guards Tank Brigade

3rd Guards Cavalry Corps
5th Guards Cavalry Division
6th Guards Cavalry Division
32nd Guards Cavalry Division

3rd Guards Mechanised Corps
7th Guards Mechanised Brigade
8th Guards Mechanised Brigade
35th Guards Mechanised Brigade

1st Air Army

1st Guards Bomber Corps
3rd Guards Bomber Aviation Division
4th Guards Bomber Aviation Division
5th Guards Bomber Aviation Division
6th Guards Bomber Aviation Division
113th Guards Bomber Aviation Division
334th Guards Bomber Aviation Division
213th Guards Bomber Aviation Division

[includes Fighter Aviation Corps]

2nd Byelorussian Front

33rd Army

62nd Rifle Corps
70th Rifle Division
157th Rifle Division
344th Rifle Division

49th Army

62nd Rifle Corps
64th Rifle Division
330th Rifle Division
369th Rifle Division

69th Rifle Corps
42nd Rifle Division
222nd Rifle Division

76th Rifle Corps
49th Rifle Division
199th Rifle Division
290th Rifle Division

81st Rifle Corps
32nd Rifle Division
95th Rifle Division
153rd Rifle Division
42nd Guards Tank Brigade
43rd Guards Tank Brigade

50th Army

19th Rifle Corps
324th Rifle Division
362nd Rifle Division

38th Rifle Corps
110th Rifle Division
139th Rifle Division
385th Rifle Division

121st Rifle Corps
238th Rifle Division
307th Rifle Division
380th Rifle Division

[includes the 4th Air Army]

1st Byelorussian Front

4th Artillery Corps

5th Artillery Division
12th Artillery Division

3rd Army

35th Rifle Corps
250th Rifle Division

323rd Rifle Division
348th Rifle Division

40th Rifle Corps
120th Guards Rifle Division
269th Guards Rifle Division

41st Rifle Corps
129th Rifle Division
169th Rifle Division

46th Rifle Corps
82nd Rifle Division
108th Rifle Division
413th Rifle Division

80th Rifle Corps
5th Rifle Division
186th Rifle Division
283rd Rifle Division

9th Tank Corps
23rd Tank Brigade
95th Tank Brigade
108th Tank Brigade
8th Mechanised Brigade

Army Artillery
5 Guards Mortar Division

28th Army

3rd Guards Rifle Corps
50th Guards Rifle Division
54th Guards Rifle Division
96th Guards Rifle Division

20th Rifle Corps
48th Guards Rifle Division
55th Guards Rifle Division
20th Rifle Division

128th Rifle Corps
61st Rifle Division
130th Rifle Division
152nd Rifle Division

Army Artillery
5th Breakthrough Artillery Division
12th Breakthrough Artillery Division

48th Army

29th Rifle Corps
102nd Rifle Division
217th Rifle Division

42nd Rifle Corps
137th Rifle Division
170th Rifle Division
399th Rifle Division

53rd Rifle Corps
17th Rifle Division
73rd Rifle Division
96th Rifle Division
194th Rifle Division

Army Artillery
22nd Breakthrough Artillery Division

61st Army

9th Guards Rifle Corps
12th Guards Rifle Division
212th Rifle Division

89th Rifle Corps
23rd Rifle Division
55th Rifle Division
397th Rifle Division
415th Rifle Division

65th Army

18th Rifle Corps
37th Guards Rifle Division
44th Guards Rifle Division
69th Rifle Division

105th Rifle Corps
75th Guards Rifle Division
15th Rifle Division
193rd Rifle Division
354th Rifle Division
356th Rifle Division

1st Guards Tank Corps
1st Guards Mechanised Brigade
15th Guards Tank Brigade
16th Guards Tank Brigade
17th Guards Tank Brigade

1st Mechanised Corps
19th Mechanised Brigade
35th Mechanised Brigade
37th Mechanised Brigade
219th Tank Brigade

Army Artillery
26th Artillery Division

Front Units

2nd Guards Cavalry Corps
3rd Guards Cavalry Division
4th Guards Cavalry Division
17th Guards Cavalry Division

4th Guards Cavalry Corps
9th Guards Cavalry Division
10th Guards Cavalry Division
30th Guards Cavalry Division

7th Guards Cavalry Corps
14th Guards Cavalry Division
15th Guards Cavalry Division
16th Guards Cavalry Division

Dnepr Combat Flotilla
1st Riverine Brigade
2nd Riverine Brigade
3rd Riverine Brigade

[includes 6th & 16th Air Army & independent units]

APPENDIX VI

Army Group Centre Order of Battle 15 July 1944

SECOND ARMY

Reserves
5th Hungarian Reserve Division
23rd Hungarian Reserve Division
1st Hungarian Cavalry Division
52nd Security Division

XX Army Corps
3rd Cavalry Brigade
March Battalion of 7th Infantry Division 35th Infantry Division (in transit)

XXIII Army Corps
292nd Infantry Division
102nd Infantry Division

LV Army Corps
28th Jäger Division
367th Infantry Division
12th Panzer Division
part of 20th Panzer Division (*Kampfgruppe* Demme)

Group Harteneck
4th Panzer Division
4th Cavalry Brigade
part of 129th Infantry Division

FOURTH ARMY

VI Army Corps
50th Infantry Division
5th Panzer Division
Group Florke
Group Gottberg

XXXIX Panzer Corps
remnants of 221st Security Division
131st Infantry Division
170th Infantry Division
7th Panzer Division

THIRD PANZER ARMY

XXVI Army Corps
201st Security Division
Kampfgruppe 6th Panzer Division
March Battalion 69
parts of 196th Infantry Division

IX Army Corps
212th Infantry Division
March Battalion 252nd Infantry Division
parts of 391st Security Division
Panzergrenadier Brigade von Werthern

XXVI Army Corps
parts of 134th Infantry Division
parts of 299th Infantry Division
parts of 337th Infantry Division
parts of 383rd Infantry Division

XII Army Corps
Panzergrenadier Division 'Feldherrnhalle'
18th Panzergrenadier Division
6th Infantry Division
12th Infantry Division
31st Infantry Division
36th Infantry Division
45th Infantry Division
57th Infantry Division
267th Infantry Division
296th Infantry Division

XXV Army Corps
390th Security Division
707th Infantry Division

LIII Army Corps
4th Luftwaffe Field Division
6th Luftwaffe Field Division
14th Infantry Division
206th Infantry Division
246th Infantry Division
286th Security Division

APPENDIX VII

Army Group Centre Order of Battle 19 July 1944

SECOND ARMY

XX Army Corps

7th Infantry Division
242nd Security Battalion
258th Security Battalion
315th Security Battalion
3rd Cavalry Brigade
930th Security Regiment
42nd Jäger Division

XXIII Army Corps

102nd Infantry Division with remains of 7th Infantry Division
292nd Infantry Division
1st Battalion Hungarian Infantry Regiment 46
Panzer Jäger Abteilung 66
Group Harteneck
Group Merker

LV Army Corps

remnants 1st Hungarian Cavalry Division
remnants 35th Infantry Division

FOURTH ARMY

Recce Btn 19th Panzer Division
Recce Btn 20th Panzer Division
Group Gottberg
Blocking Group Weidling
Group Florke
remnants 14th Infantry Division
50th Infantry Division with Artillery Rgt 12th Panzer Division

THIRD PANZER ARMY

Group Tolsdorf

IX Corps

Regiment Group 347 with 2nd Battalion 197th Infantry Division
Blocking Group Rothkirch
206th Infantry Division
245th Infantry Division
4th Luftwaffe Field Division
6th Luftwaffe Field Division
286th Security Division

Table of Ranks

German Army	Waffen-SS	British Army
Gemeiner, Landser	Schütze	Private
—	Oberschütze	—
Grenadier	Sturmmann	Lance Corporal
Obergrenadier	—	—
Gefreiter	Rottenführer	Corporal
Obergefreiter	Unterscharführer	—
Stabsgefreiter	—	—
Unteroffizier	Scharführer	Sergeant
Unterfeldwebel	Oberscharführer	Colour Sergeant
Feldwebel	—	—
Oberfeldwebel	Hauptscharführer	Sergeant Major
Stabsfeldwebel	Hauptbereitschaftsleiter	—
—	Sturmscharführer	Warrant Officer
Leutnant	Untersturmführer	Second Lieutenant
Oberleutnant	Obersturmführer	First Lieutenant
Hauptmann	Hauptsturmführer	Captain
Major	Sturmbannführer	Major
Oberstleutnant	Obersturmbannführer	Lieutenant Colonel
Oberst	Standartenführer	Colonel
—	Oberführer	Brigadier General
Generalmajor	Brigadeführer	Major General
Generalleutnant	Gruppenführer	Lieutenant General
General	Obergruppenführer	General
Generaloberst	Oberstgruppenführer	—
Generalfeldmarschall	Reichsführer-SS	—

Bibliography

Documents

9th Army, Fuhrungsabteilung, Kriegstagebuch Nr.10, 22 Juni 1944, 9th Army files 59691/10, 69402/I, 64802/I

Gr. Mitte, an den Chef des Gen StdH, 10.07.44, H. Gr. Mitte, Ia Akte V, H. Gr Mitte files 65004/18, 63015/I, 64190/4

H.Gr. Mitte, Ia Kriegstagebuch, 1 – 31.07.44 OCMH files

Kriegstagebuch der 3. Panzer-Armee

Kriegstagebuch der 4. Armee

Kriegstagebuch der 2. Armee

Published Works

Brehm, W., *Mein Kriegstagebuch 1939- 1945. Mit der 7. Panzer-Division, 5 Jahre in West und Ost*, Kassel, privately published, 1953

Dethleffsen, *Heeresgruppe Mitte, Das 39. Panzer-Korps unter General de Artillerie Martinek 1942 – 1944, Der Rückzugskampf von Rschew bis zur Beresina*, Wien, n.d.

Haupt, W., *Heeresgruppe Mitte*, Dorheim, Podzun, 1968

Hinze, R., *Der Zusammenbuch der Heeresgruppe Mitte in Osten 1944*, Stuttgart, Motorbuch Verlag, 1980

Hinze, R., *Die 19. Panzer-Division*, Friedberg/Hessen, privately published, 1982

Merker, L., *Das Buch der 78. Sturm-Division*, Tübingen, Kameradenhilfswerk, 1955

Paul, W., *Brennpunkte, Geschichte der 6. Panzer-Division,*

Saucken, D. von, *4. Panzer-Division*, Coburg, Traditionsverband der Division, 1968

Scheele, *Geschichte der 19. Panzer-Division, Mitte Julis bis 5.11.44*, Geilenkirchen, 1976

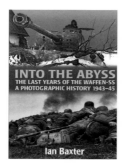

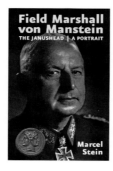